CUT
THE
STRINGS

CUT THE STRINGS

SHARON CAVERS

AMY JACKSON

GARDEN PATH INSPIRATIONS & PUBLISHING

Garden Path Inspirations & Publishing
Cavan, Ontario
L0A 1C0 Canada
www.gardenpathinspirations.com

Author photos by Craig Foster. Copy editing by Marcia Laycock
Cover photo, design and typesetting by pagedesign.ca

Some names have been changed to preserve their anonymity.

Library and Archives Canada Cataloguing in Publication

Cavers, Sharon
Cut the strings / Sharon Cavers, Amy Jackson.

Includes bibliographical references.
ISBN 978-0-9866307-0-5

1. Cavers, Sharon. 2. Jackson, Amy Ruth. 3. Mothers and daughters—
Ontario—Biography. 4. Drug addicts—Family relationships—Ontario.
5. Alcoholics—Family relationships—Ontario. 6. Drug abuse—Religious
aspects—Christianity. 7. Alcoholism—Religious aspects—Christianity.
8. Spiritual healing. I. Jackson, Amy Ruth II. Title.

HV5805.C39A3 2010   362.29092   C2010-903651-4

WHAT READERS ARE SAYING ABOUT CUT THE STRINGS

"Anyone who has lived with and prayed for a prodigal child will relate to this story. Told with honesty and vulnerability, Sharon and Amy both allow us into their lives as they struggle toward hope and healing. We ache and rejoice with them as they learn to trust in the mercy and grace of a God who never abandons them."

—Marcia Laycock
Award-winning author

"A wonderful story! Beautifully written! Powerful! Anointed! I couldn't put it down. I felt God's Holy Spirit continually throughout the entire story saying, Get this out there. So many need this."

—Pastor Maureen Patrick
Director of Pastoral Care,
Calvary Pentecostal Church

"This book is a graphic and honest portrayal of an intense journey with a "prodigal" child. Throughout the "journey" we continue to see the steadfast faithfulness of God. We are constantly reminded that He is in control; at *all* times; and of *all* things. The level of honesty and transparency by both authors is gripping and humbling. This is a *must read* for anyone facing this situation."

—Linda McLean
Friend and Encourager

"Thank you on behalf of all the parents and their children who will read your story and be comforted, convicted or changed by it. What a wonderful testimony of God's grace and strength and faithfulness. Many times I wept as I read and many times I jumped for joy. The story flowed seamlessly and I felt I couldn't put it down. This has encouraged me that God is always at work and always in control. God's Spirit is alive in this story."

—Sherri Spence-Lichty
Mentoring Program Director,
Kawartha Youth for Christ

To our Lord and Saviour
Jesus Christ, ·
whose unfailing love
inspired us to share our story.

To our husbands,
Bill and Stephen,
the loves of our lives.

In memory of Madeline Cox,
beloved Mother and praying Grandmother

CONTENTS

ACKNOWLEDGEMENTS

To our Lord and Saviour, Jesus Christ. Our story is the story of your faithfulness.

A special thanks to Julie and Michelle for giving valuable feedback on the early chapters. Your enthusiasm spurred us on to finish the book.

We couldn't have written this book without the support of our husbands, Bill and Stephen. Your love enabled us to be transparent and write honestly. Thanks for understanding when you had to watch all those hockey games alone while we were writing.

Our love and gratitude to Pastor David Mainse. We are honoured to have you write the foreword for our book. Your faithful teaching of God's Word when I was a young girl greatly contributed to the strong foundation of faith upon which I have built my life. I hold you and Norma-Jean in high esteem.

To the members of The Writer's Crucible group who provided valuable assistance in critiquing some of the first chapters. Thanks for your words of wisdom and advice. You are the best.

Thanks to our close friends who believed in us and cheered us on from the moment we said "yes" to God to the completion of our book. You will always have a special place in our hearts.

Many thanks to Marcia Laycock for her insightful editing of our manuscript.

My heart-felt thanks to the women of our prayer group who faithfully prayed for our family. The impact of your prayers may never be fully known this side of heaven. The bond between us is far greater than friendship. And for Linda, my mentor, who is now with her Lord and Saviour, I want to follow your example.

Our deepest appreciation for Pastors Frank and Maureen Patrick, dear friends and faithful servants, who teach and preach God's Word with integrity and passion. Thanks to our wonderful Calvary Church family. You are a continual blessing to our lives.

Thank you Andy and David for your artistic vision in creating a cover design that speaks without words.

FOREWORD

"Cut the Strings" tears at my heart with the extreme sadness that inflicts itself on any parent who tries to imagine what it would be like to be Amy's dad or mom. Amy's mom, Sharon, was a beautiful young girl of 9 to 12 when I had the privilege of being her Pastor. Her dad was Church Treasurer and I often visited her home getting to know one of the finest families I've ever met.

Sharon and Bill represent thousands of parents who can't even imagine that drugs, and alcohol addictions, along with sexual promiscuity could ever touch their much loved child. But it happens! And "Cut the Strings" in my judgment, is a must read in case it happens in another family. And for those in the middle of the heartbreak currently, "Cut the Strings" will give a vital "How to cope and how to overcome" plan.

Finally, I love happy endings. Don't you? Thanks for the honour of participating in your most important ministry.

David Mainse
Founder, Crossroads Christian Communications Inc. & Crossroads Television System (CTS)

PROLOGUE

Amy

Words, it all started with words. Lying to myself, lying about myself, lying about what I had or had not tried. What I did or did not like. Saying things that I knew weren't right. The Devil[1] unleashed his arrows. I began rationalizing my lies, because, after all, lies are *just* words not actions. What does it matter if I say I've smoked weed? I know I haven't, wouldn't it be much worse if I was getting high? The arrows penetrate, but I leave them there pretending they don't hurt.

I start thinking that if I do some of the things I've lied about then they won't be lies. The only way to stop the lies is to stop lying and start doing. The wounds from the arrows begin to fester and swell. I justify my actions by telling myself it's not who I really am. If I have a few drinks every now and again, I'm not a drunk. It just becomes a means to an end, an end of the lies. Isn't it better to be truthful and misguided for a short time, than to become a lying hypocrite? I mean, if I say I'm doing something I might just as well do it. The poison from the arrow slowly works deeper and deeper into the open wound.

It's not that I don't know I need to stop; it's that I don't remember why I wanted to. I mean, if you're going to do something you should do it all the way, right? Stop living two lives, pretending to be some good upright person that I'm not. Nobody likes a faker. I validate the garbage in my life by telling myself that it's just who I am, and who I want to be. The infection spreads into my bloodstream and through my body. Death is imminent.

Sharon

There are moments in life when you feel like you've been kicked in the stomach so hard you double over as all the breath rushes out of your body. Your head reels. Darkness washes over you like a black, viscous wave. You try to stand, but your knees buckle and you slump to the floor. January 17, 2004 was one of those days.

It's Sunday morning. I awake with a pounding headache, feeling nauseous, aching all over, my body hot with fever. The flu virus has found another victim to invade. Pulling the covers closer, I try to get comfortable as my husband, Bill, dresses for church. I have a fleeting thought that I could use the hours while the house is quiet to read my Bible and listen to worship music. It vanishes when I realize I can't lift my head off the pillow. I know God's presence will be with me here as surely as it will be with all who gather together for praise and worship this morning.

We think nothing of hearing a car pull into our driveway. Our youngest daughter, Amy, spent the night at a friend's house. I breathe a sigh of relief that she has arrived home safely. Her nights out with friends, once occasional, now are a weekend habit.

Last evening, as she got ready to leave, I wanted to call out to her and suggest she ask Jenn to pick her up instead of driving herself, but what reason would I give for this intrusion into her life. She wasn't sixteen with a new driver's licence. She'd been driving for three years. The weather was clear and no snow storms were forecast to cause concern. Why then this churning in my stomach and pounding of my heart?

I slept poorly, awakening several times in the night feeling a strong impression to pray for Amy. *Where were they going? They might start out at Jenn's house, but where would they end up?*

My head throbs, and my stomach rolls. I'm not a good patient. I'd rather be up getting ready for church. I hear a car door slam. *Why is she returning so early in the morning?* Usually she comes home after we have left for church. I hear her saying good-bye to someone. "Why is she being dropped off at his hour? Why didn't she drive her own car home?" I ask. My husband goes to find out.

From the bedroom, I hear their voices in the hallway, conversation rising and falling like waves crashing on a rocky shore. I hear crying. It can't be Amy; she's too tough to cry.

When they come into the bedroom, I can tell something is terribly wrong. Our daughter's face is a mask of misery and shame. She bows her head. My heart and head are pounding in the same rhythm. Time is suspended while we wait for her to speak.

ONE

BEGINNINGS

Sharon

I remember the day as if it were yesterday. Sitting on the sofa beside my husband I waited nervously, hardly daring to breathe as he opened the gift. It was our eleventh anniversary. Bill tore away the paper and stared questioningly at the small card inside the box. It simply read: "I am pregnant. Happy Anniversary. Sherry." It was his pet name for me when we were dating. A huge smile covered his face as he wrapped his arms around me and hugged me tightly. It was hard to tell who was more excited about the news.

A family of four never seemed complete to me. Our two daughters, seven-year-old Julie and four-year-old Michelle were as different as day and night. Julie, serious, thoughtful and always eager to obey, enjoyed being the older sister. Michelle's personality tipped the other end of the scale with her dare-devil approach to everything and a stubborn will that challenged even the simplest of rules.

Sometimes God tells us things in the most unexpected ways. One morning while Michelle was absorbed in building a tower of blocks, I opened my Bible to 2 Kings where I had been reading the day before and found a beautiful story of hospitality and unexpected blessing. A Shunammite woman was in the habit of preparing a meal for Elisha and his servant every time they traveled by her home. She asked her husband if they might prepare a small room on the roof for the man of God.

She and her elderly husband opened their home and their hearts and provided for the needs of Elisha and his servant, Gehazi. Elisha asked his servant what could be done for this caring and compassionate woman who had been so kind to them. As I continued reading, one verse stood out even though I must have read it many times before.

"About this time next year," Elisha said, "you will hold a son in your arms."[2] It seemed God was speaking these words directly to me. I cherished them and held them in my heart as a precious promise.

A son. Could it be true? Throughout my pregnancy, I pondered the verse. I began to understand that God wanted me to rejoice over the baby growing inside me and not be concerned over the sex of this child. Some days I was convinced I was carrying a girl, and other days I felt just as sure it was a boy.

On one of those days I bought a small blue sweater and bonnet. I tucked it away in a drawer filled with the distinctive fragrance of baby soap. I listened politely to predictions from family and friends, all the while knowing God would decide whether a son or another daughter would complete our family.

I smiled at God's tender care. I had already prayed for a healthy child, but now I asked my heavenly Father for two special things. First that this baby would be smaller than our other two daughters who weighed in at eight pounds two ounces, and nine pounds seven ounces respectively. My obstetrician seemed a bit concerned when he announced at one of my prenatal visits that this baby was much smaller than the other two. I simply smiled and said nothing.

The second request was basically selfish. I prayed that I would experience the excitement of rushing to the hospital in the middle of the night. Since my first two children had both been born by cesarean section, this pregnancy would follow the same path. Our child's birth date was set for December 29. I would be admitted to the hospital early in the morning for blood work.

Imagine my joy when I experienced labor pains for the very first time on December 16—almost two weeks before I was scheduled to go to the hospital. Bill returned home from a church board meeting to find me packing a small suitcase. Never having felt contractions before, I could only assume the persistent and equally timed pains meant our baby was on the way.

Bill's mother, Jean, graciously got out of bed at 1:00 a.m. and came to stay with our girls. I was thrilled to have my husband rush me to the emergency department of our local hospital in the middle of the night, suitcase in hand, and giggling. God knows the deepest desires of our hearts, and on this occasion, he delighted in granting one of mine.

The excitement was cut short when I reached the admitting desk. At first, the admissions nurse treated me like any other pregnant woman, fussing over me and asking how far apart my contractions were coming. But when she discovered that I had been booked for a cesarean section between Christmas and New Year's, things changed abruptly.

My obstetrician arrived looking less than pleased. After a quick examination, he announced the ominous news that my contractions must be stopped. In his brusque manner he assured me this would not harm my baby in any way. In the short time since my arrival, I had somehow become an inconvenience, a schedule-disrupter! What could I possibly disrupt in a maternity ward where babies are delivered around the clock?

My joy plummeted. I had upset the order of things by arriving too early, as if I had a choice in the matter. I wanted to argue, but what could I say to these professionals? A young nurse strapped a fetal monitor to my belly. Before I could ask any questions, the obstetrician gave me a quick explanation and administered medication to stop the contractions.

Everything happened in a whirlwind of activity. The doctor advised Bill to go home. I would be kept overnight and my labor monitored. When the contractions continued, I heard the frustration in the obstetrician's voice as he directed an orderly to move me quickly to an operating room.

I found out later that my dear husband had just arrived home on that snowy December night when the call from the nurse sent him racing back to the hospital. He waited anxiously in the hallway while the surgeon performed a cesarean section and delivered our beautiful seven pound, eight ounce daughter. Hearing the news that mom and baby were okay helped to assuage the anger he felt at not being called back in time to be with me for her birth.

The nurse lifted her up for me to see, but because of the epidural I was not permitted to hold my darling daughter. She would not feel the warmth of my arms or the comfort of my breast for many hours. I remembered looking into her tiny face and wondering if we had bonded. I felt the separation keenly. Pushing doubts aside, I rejoiced and thanked God for her safe delivery.

On the Sunday of her dedication, she wore the blue sweater over a frilly white dress. As we had with each of our children, we took seriously the commitment we were making to raise her in the ways of God and to pray earnestly for her until she could make her own decision to serve him.

We accepted the responsibility of training her in God's Word and setting a godly example for her with his help and to the best of our ability. The congregation stood in agreement with us, promising to encourage and pray for our daughter. On that day, we gave her back into God's hands, asking him to fulfill his perfect will and plan for her life. When God gives a gift it not only blesses the one receiving it, but has far reaching blessings for many others as well. I knew this child would bring so much more than completion to our family.

What would life hold for Amy, whose name means Beloved of God?

I didn't know then that God would direct my thoughts back to this memorable day at a time when my heart was overflowing with pain and a violent storm raged around us. The truth that we had placed our daughter into the hands of God became my secure anchor.

TWO

CHANGES

Sharon

A mother-daughter relationship is unique among relationships. Being of the same gender one might suppose that there would be a greater understanding for each other, similarity of thought, ideals and goals. But Amy and I were quite different. I have a sanguine temperament and she is strongly choleric. Sanguines tend to be friendly, spontaneous and compassionate while cholerics are strong-willed, decisive and capable.[3] In general terms each of us is a mix of personality traits. God in his wisdom did not create any two people exactly alike.

As a parent you always want the best for your children. You love them, nurture them, teach, discipline and guide them, endeavoring most of all to instill truths, values, and beliefs that will lead them to a personal relationship with God—a relationship that will be their anchor when the storms of life hit them in the face.

I remembered watching Amy go through all the phases of childhood. She always wanted to try new things, be independent and do everything her own way. Though not openly rebellious, she found ways to exercise her independent nature.

Her love for animals found expression in caring for creatures of all sorts—turtles, hamsters, snails, baby birds that had fallen from nests, and finally a lovable cat named Sydney. But more than anything, Amy loved horses.

When she wanted to take riding lessons, we agreed to pay half of the cost if she mowed the lawn to earn the rest. She told us that she planned to own a horse of her own someday and participate in equestrian riding competitions. With her drive and determination we never doubted she would accomplish her dreams.

In Grade eight, Amy experienced the humiliation of being fitted with glasses and braces in the same month. She chose blue frames, but later complained the glasses made her look worse and drew more attention to her. Like most kids with glasses, she endured the jokes and teasing. She admitted that wearing her fluorescent retainer was the only positive thing about the whole braces experience. We tried to make her feel good about how she looked, but she always seemed to be trying to prove something to herself and to us. I saw it as normal adolescent behaviour but an inkling of doubt settled in my mind.

I heard a comedian say, "Once we had our third child, there were more of them than us." It made me wonder if we made the mistake of overlooking things with Amy that later became problems because we were busy coping with the stress and concerns that raising two other teenage daughters presented.

Throughout her early teenage years, Amy still said what she knew we wanted to hear, and most often did the right things. We attended church as a family, though more and more she said she wasn't feeling well and stayed home. She lost interest in The Escape, the youth group at our church, citing cliquish behaviour as the reason. Although we prayed with her and encouraged her to trust God during this difficult time, she never went back.

We prayed continually for our girls, knowing the normal struggles of growing up were as difficult for them as ours had been for us during our teenage years. Her sisters had faced peer pressure and problems too, but were blessed with a few good friends over the years. Amy never really found a true friend in the church family. Perhaps she kept would-be friends at arm's length.

Amy

I guess I thought being a Christian meant believing, believing in everything; God, Jesus, his death on the cross. I knew it was all true, never doubted it. Never connected that I was a sinner going to hell. I needed to talk to Jesus one-on-one. I needed his blood to cover *my* sins, sins I didn't even know I had. Simple belief in him wasn't enough.

Maybe that's why youth group was never anything more to me than something to do on a Friday night. Some place to go, people to hang with. I can recall few memories from those years, but the ones that I can are vivid.

One Friday night, after our youth pastor finished talking he gave an invitation to come forward for those who wanted to pray and receive prayer. I made my way up to the front and knelt down. There were so many things on my mind. I was confused and depressed from places deep within me. As I knelt I waited for someone to come and pray for me. I needed someone to put an arm round my shoulder, someone to sit with me. My feelings of sadness grew stronger, and tears started to run down my face.

No one came. I could hear people beginning to talk and laugh as the night drew to an end. My heart ached with loneliness. As I dried my tears with my shirt sleeve I wondered why no one came. The only conclusion I could draw was that no one cared. These friends that I thought I had, friends who loved God and sincerely loved each other, were fakes. They were no different than the jerks and snobs at school. The realization hurt me deeply. I left early that night and decided then that I didn't need to go back. I got enough emotional pain from school. I didn't want more.

If only I could have seen then that I was not alone. God himself sat with me and cried with me. His heart ached with mine. His loving arms were around me, never to let me go.

THREE

CHAMELEON

Sharon

Amy moved through all the grades of public school with the same group of girls from our neighborhood. Though these ties were never completely broken in high school, she renewed them now with an obvious enthusiasm. Somehow we failed to see the signs that she was drifting away from us. Captivated by friends who represented a lifestyle she was eager to know more about, her heart slowly turned away from God.

One day while putting her pay stubs in her filing cabinet drawer, I found some small clay pipes which I assumed were her latest expressions of creativity. For several weeks I had noticed a green leaf attached to her key chain. I thought nothing of it until one of her friends commented on the cool marijuana leaf. When I asked her about it she laughed and said it was nothing—a decoration—no big deal!

Trust has always been a high priority in our home. We have chosen to trust each other and believe that what we hear is the truth until proven otherwise. When I confronted Amy and asked if she were doing drugs, she said "no" in a very convincing manner. Naive as it may sound, I believed her.

I saw none of the tell tale signs—no radical change in personality or behaviour, decreased appetite or noticeable change in weight or depression, and her grades at school hadn't changed. I'd often done a load of her laundry when she worked long hours at a ranch and never once found a telltale joint or baggie full of suspicious leaves in her pockets. Perhaps the marijuana leaf was for attention. Teens have a way of saying and doing things just to drive their parents crazy with worry. Some of these are harmless. Most are not! But deep in my heart I knew something was wrong—very, very wrong.

Amy

I guess it started for me when I learned to care more about what others thought of me than what I thought of myself. I was so preoccupied with how they would view me that I didn't even stop to think about what I was doing. Being around them was fun, having friends to hang out with was fun. I was more than willing to bend a little for the sake of friendship.

So I started liking what they liked, laughing at what they laughed at. I became a chameleon. I blended in. Who I was on the outside didn't match the inside. I tried hard to be stronger, quicker, tougher, so that the true me wouldn't show through. If they could do it, then I could do it better. No matter what the "it" was.

Being so absorbed with the fact that I *could*, I didn't stop to think if I *should*. It seemed logical to me. After all, if I didn't start doing what I said I was doing then I would be a fake, and nobody likes a phony. I felt I needed to at least back up my claims, if only for the time being. So I smoked a little weed, had the odd cigarette. I thought I liked the feeling of being numb to the world, but in reality I was trying harder than ever to fit in.

I knew deep down this wasn't me, but it became exciting to meet new people, and try new things. I had grown very attached to my friends, and cared for them deeply. It was fun hanging out. We got together, got high, ate chips and played video games. Before long I had formed a regular routine, and I liked it.

⊱ FOUR ⊰

FEARS EXPOSED

Sharon

For many people January 1, 2000 dawned in a black cloud of fear. The media warned us for months prior to December 31 that the Millennium Bug—Y2K—would strike at midnight throwing the world into chaos. Banks and government offices would cease operating. Threats of worldwide computer break-downs, water shortages and extensive power failures headlined the daily news.

We were urged to store drinking water, stockpile food supplies and fill our bathtubs with water on New Year's Eve. Some fear mongers went so far as to suggest we purchase firearms to protect our loved ones and ward off looters.

Bill and I listened to all the predictions and made our decision. We purchased some extra canned foods and filled a few large bottles with water in the event there might be a short power cut. On New Year's Eve, we enjoyed an evening walk and shared communion together. Before we went to bed we prayed for God's provision and protection.

Gradually the world became aware that nothing disastrous had happened. Lights stayed on, water flowed from taps and appliances worked. Life returned to normal with endless discussions as to whether Y2K was a hoax or simply an error in judgement.

Sometimes it is easier to trust God in the big things and fail miserably at trusting him in the smaller circumstances of life. Trust and fear cannot co-exist. I could trust God for whatever would happen in the New Year, but I had many fears buried beneath the surface of my life.

God used a neighborhood dog to expose a deeply entrenched fear in my life. We have lived in our country home for 24 years among the nicest neighbours anyone could have. One blustery day as I was walking and enjoying the wintery scene left by the last snowfall, a low ominous growl stopped me in my tracks. I froze as my mind recalled a long-forgotten memory. I was nine years old, walking along a path to our neighbourhood store to buy ice cream when a large black German Sheppard knocked me to the ground. The dog stood over me snarling, the hackles on the back of his thick neck bristling. After the owner took the beast away, the sharp point of fear still pinned me to the ground.

Now many years later, I couldn't move as the dog behind me barked and inched closer. The fear that remained hidden in the basement of my heart for so long suddenly roared to life, bounded up the stairs, and smashed down the door.

Somewhere in my fear drenched mind part of a Scripture verse pushed through the panic. "When I am afraid, I will trust in you."[4] It seeped like warm liquid through my body, giving me just enough courage to walk slowly toward my house. With each step I took, the dog followed. With each tiny step, I chose trust. It wouldn't be the last time I would face this test.

Fear begins like a small seed falling into the ground. Our determination to do things our own way warms the soil. The seed is watered by the ever so gradual shifting of our trust away from God into our own abilities to handle whatever comes our way. Unseen, the roots of fear plunge deep into the fertile soil of our insecurities, into our sinful humanity. The plant that grows up, spreading its tendrils into every area of our lives, is hard to pull out. If left, its well-developed root system will become extensive and invasive.

A tiny seed of fear implanted itself in my heart on March 2, 2000. Amy got up that morning feeling sick. She admitted she'd had a drink at a friend's house and said she felt like an idiot for making that choice. She told me it was the first time she had ever tasted alcohol and promised never to drink again. I wanted to believe her, but I felt the disturbing presence of that seed of fear.

"God, keep her feet from slipping and hold her close," I prayed.

After she left for work, I went into her room and found her comforter balled up in the corner covered in vomit. Was she hoping to wash it before I saw it? When she got home, I drove her to the laundromat and waited while she washed and dried her comforter. I lectured her about the dangers of alcohol. She appeared to be listening.

Warning bells went off in my head, but I chose to ignore them. Don't most kids experiment with alcohol at some point in their teenage years, especially Christian kids who want to know what they've been missing? If it made her this sick, surely she would never drink again. Saying it and repeating it to myself make it *feel* true.

For me this discovery was the first step—the beginning of a long journey into a nightmare of darkness and pain that would be walked out a day at a time with our daughter, holding tightly to the hand of God.

Amy
Journal Entry: March 1, 2000

Tonight was awesome. Went to the bar for the first time. Lori and I went. There weren't too many people when we first got there so we sat at a table and played a drinking game. I drank her under the table. It was great. We met these two guys who were buying us drinks like all night. One of them was really cute and bonus he asked me to dance! It was crazy. The whole night all these different guys kept asking me to dance and buying me drinks. The really cute one gave me his phone number and asked me to call him tomorrow.

The best part is I saw Dave there, the same jerk that called me a dog in high school. He was hitting on me. So I asked if he remembered who I was, and when I told him he went red! I just laughed at him and walked away. It was so weird. I felt like the centre of attention. I met so many different guys, it was great. Anyway there's so much more I want to write but I don't feel so great now, so I think I'll just go to bed.

FIVE

BROKEN

Sharon

Spring had arrived. The tulips and crocuses were in full bloom. Something about this season of new life brought a fresh sense of hope. While our daughter, Michelle, was busy with preparations for her June wedding, Amy made plans to get her driver's licence. Independence shone like a beacon on the horizon. Did she realize that with greater independence came greater responsibility? Now instead of her friends driving, she would be the one behind the wheel. I panicked at the thought.

Lately Amy had been spending more and more week-ends with her friends, gradually distancing herself from our family. Returning home late on Sunday nights meant she no longer attended church with us. My journal entries were filled with prayers for our daughter, asking God to soften her heart and draw her close to himself. It was freeing to choose trust. Only then did I feel relief from the crushing weight of worry and fear. Knowing that the Good Shepherd was guarding his wandering lamb brought a measure of peace.

The bedside clock read 4:36 a.m. Something had awakened me. My husband slept soundly beside me. I quietly slid out of bed, careful not to wake him. Amy's bedroom was across the hall from ours. My steps were slow in the darkness. I reached my hand out to touch the door to her room as I had done countless times before. I pulled it back, wanting to embrace hope as long as possible. If the door resisted my touch and stayed shut, it meant Amy was home, asleep, and safe.

Tonight it swung open at the touch of my fingertips. No need to look toward the empty bed. I had the answer I came for. Fear gnawed at my heart. *Where was she tonight?* I bowed my head and prayed, "Please, God, protect her while she makes these foolish choices that can only bring her sorrow, dabbling in a lifestyle that is so dangerous both physically and spiritually." I swiped at the tears brimming in my eyes.

In the darkness accusing questions assailed me, though no voice had spoken. *What kind of a mother are you that you don't know where your daughter is? Do you really believe she'll come home? You can't control her.* Lying in bed I held my breath at the sound of every car coming down the road, my ears straining to hear tires in our driveway. "Please, Lord, let this car be Amy coming home," I pleaded, watching the headlights glide across the walls and disappear as the car passed by our house.

By 8 a.m. Amy still hadn't come home. I argued with myself about calling to find out where she'd spent the night. Maybe I should just stay out of her life. After all, she wasn't a child, she was twenty years old. In the end, fear won out. I called the friend's house where she told me she would be staying only to discover that she wasn't there.

I made an effort to keep busy, trying not to watch the hands of the clock as they ticked off each minute in their circular rotation. I stared at the phone, willing it to ring. I couldn't concentrate on the simplest of tasks. Hours later, the phone rang. I jumped at the sound even though I'd been waiting for it, longing for it. Amy's voice sounded distant. Before I could ask, she told me she was with another friend, and everything was okay. Her tone made it clear the conversation was over.

When she finally arrived home in the afternoon, I was more than ready to talk. Something had to change. The occasional nights out with friends had gradually turned into a predictable pattern of being out every weekend. Amy was sliding farther and farther down a slippery slope that lead to heartache and despair.

When she started dating Chris a few years ago, we were pleased that he came from a Christian home. He was respectful, had good manners and got along well with our family. We knew his parents, and it was obvious that Amy really loved this guy.

I soon saw telltale signs of trouble in their relationship, but Amy chose not to talk to us about it. I often saw her in tears. Was this the reason she turned to her friends? The more the relationship failed, the harder she tried to be someone else.

Amy

I've heard parents say that teenagers don't know what love is, that they are not capable of *real love.* I think that's completely false. We may not understand the sensible, intelligent and realistic side of love, but the feelings and emotions are intact and thriving. When I was about fifteen I fell in love with a boy I worked with. I was in love with Chris secretly for years before we got together. Thinking of him constantly left little room in my life for anything else.

All that I cared about was how he would see me. I was always trying to prove myself to him. Prove that I was pretty enough, smart enough, tough enough, funny enough. Being just Amy was never good enough for me. When he asked me out I finally felt wanted by someone. I walked away from God and into Chris' arms. I lived on my intense feelings of love, and happiness. Nothing else was important to me.

After three years it ended. My heart was broken into pieces so small I thought they could never be put back together. I had no feelings of love, joy or happiness left. I was like an empty shell. I'd fixed my thoughts on him, and now he was gone. My life was consumed by us, but now it was just me. Just me was never good enough. Sadness overwhelmed me and I knew I would never be the same. I didn't realize that I had removed God from my heart and tried to replace the hole with a boyfriend. All I knew was my heart ached deeply.

Sharon
Journal Entry: June 6, 2000

Amy is broken-hearted. Her world came crashing down when she and Chris broke up. When she talked about him it was evident by the excitement in her voice and the look in her eyes that she was serious about this guy. Now she has put up the walls and won't let us into her world. She slips on her mask of confidence and continues to put on a brave front. I see the pain on her face and pray she will run into the arms of God for comfort and guidance rather than sink deeper into the lifestyle she's dabbling in. I long to talk with her but she has withdrawn and chooses to bear her pain alone.

Journal Entry: June 10, 2000

Amy tells me that she hasn't been going to the bars for about a month and a half. This is a wonderful answer to prayer whether she realizes it or not. Father, only your love can reach our wayward daughter. Her ears are closed to our words. I pray they are not closed to your voice. Please, help her to see her great need of you. She will continue to fail on her own. Life has become a roller coaster of emotions. We see answers to prayer and rejoice. The roller coaster climbs higher.

Journal entry: June 26, 2000

We found out today that our daughter is back at the bars. She went on the weekend and had some drinks. Today she told me she found it boring and not as much fun anymore. I'm not sure it's the truth. The roller coaster plummets downward. Our hopes are shattered once again. The enemy is working hard to destroy our daughter, but I believe with all my heart God will be victorious in the end. Tears are blinding my eyes as I write these words. I write them with more faith than I feel.

Journal Entry: September 4, 2000

Amy tells me that she seriously wants to change her life. She is not making this decision to please us, but because she knows it's right and she's seeing how hollow and unsatisfying her life is. My heart leaps with joy at her words. I pray God will prevent the enemy from drawing her away from this decision. *Please, Lord, give her the strength and help she needs to follow through with resolve.* The roller coaster climbs again.

Journal Entry: December 3, 2000

Amy is out all night with one of her friends. The roller coaster careens wildly downward. It is painful to watch someone you love choosing to listen to Satan's lies. Amy is trying so hard to be anything but average—to be something special—stronger, faster, smarter. If only she could understand that she doesn't have to prove anything. God, you love her just the way she is. Has the enemy completely blinded her to your love and truth?

Journal Entry: December 16, 2000

Amy arrived home, said nothing, and went to bed. It is too painful to write more. We have talked with her, counseled her, cried for her, and prayed for her. Lord, we need your wisdom. In the tumult of my emotions I hear you say to my heart, *Peace, be still.*

SIX

CONFRONTATION

Sharon

The New Year 2001 began with a wonderful reminder of God's faithfulness. My dad found and returned to me a book I had given to my mom when she and my sister were going through some dark days. "For The Love of My Daughter", by Mary Ellen Ton, was an encouragement to her many years ago. Now, it encouraged me as I read it again while I walked through my own difficult days with Amy.

God used it to remind me that he was working in our children's lives in ways we couldn't always see. If we truly trusted him, and let them go, he would accomplish his will in their lives. What a blessed assurance this became for a mother who was feeling hurt and confused.

During these days, we had not shared with many of our friends the day to day struggles we were dealing with. After all, I reasoned, most parents encounter problems with their teens and young adults as they become independent and choose their own way. Why burden others with our problems?

Turning to Pastor Maureen as my confidante, I often sought her out to share the pain in my heart. I knew she would understand. We had prayed for each other's children over the years and watched as God directed their steps and revealed his plans and purposes for their lives. Her hugs and wise counsel stilled my anxious thoughts.

I saw a cartoon that depicted people going into a church service. As they walked through the door, they took off their masks and dropped them into a basket. A sign attached to it read: Deposit masks here. I wanted to drop my 'everything's fine with us' façade, but the embarrassment I felt kept my mask firmly in place.

It hurt me deeply when several of our friends in the family of God came to us with the news that Amy was frequenting the bars downtown. There seemed to be more satisfaction than compassion in bringing us this news. I felt like asking them how they knew the information they were so eager to share, but instead I listened politely as they talked, all the time wanting to scream, "Have you prayed for us?"

I think they expected me to be shocked—a good Christian girl in a bar! They were surprised when I told them we already knew. One thing our daughter didn't do was to hide this part of her life from us. If she wasn't hiding that, was there something else she was hiding? My questions to her usually brought vague answers.

One evening things came to a head. I don't remember what sparked the conversation we had that snowy January night, but I will never forget the impact it had on all of us. As we sat around the kitchen table talking with Amy, we began to ask questions. I didn't expect her to open up, but little by little she began to tell us about her life. At one point I asked, "Is there anything else we should know?" all the while hoping the answer would be "no".

We learned that our daughter had been smoking marijuana for a year, but she assured us that she had never used drugs in our home or on our property. Small consolation, yet I appreciated her honesty. I felt naive and betrayed. The little clay pipe I'd found in her drawer did mean something after all.

Bill and I knew the time had come to take a difficult step for a parent. Our daughter was 21 and still living at home. I heard a retreat speaker describe how an eagle will begin to make the nest more and more uncomfortable when she knows it's time for her eaglets to leave their home and learn to fly.

She stirs up the nest causing twigs and sharp sticks to poke out of their soft feather-lined bed. She flaps her wings at them. Soon the young eagles find the only comfortable place to sit is on the edge of the nest. Mother eagle is telling them it's time to try their wings.

Amy worked two part-time jobs and we enjoyed having her at home. We couldn't see the sense in her spending money on an apartment she didn't need, and she agreed. However, the time had come to make the comfy home nest a lot less comfortable.

I remembered hearing Dr. James Dobson say: "Don't throw away your friendship over behavior that has no great moral significance. There will be plenty of real issues that require you to stand like a rock. Save your big guns for those crucial confrontations."[5]

We were about to have one of those confrontations. Bill explained the rules under which she could stay, but made it clear she could not continue her involvement in illegal activities. If she wished to continue the life she had chosen, she would have to find some place else to live. We both assured her our door would always be open for her to come home. Even as we uttered those words, I sensed the enemy rubbing his hands with glee, thinking he'd gained a great victory. It was the hardest thing we had ever done.

"We'll give you two weeks to make a decision," my husband said. I held my breath, waiting for her to say something. I thought she would hear the thumping of my heart. Tears crept into my eyes. I could hardly breathe around the lump in my throat. I never imagined we would say those words to one of our daughters. *Were we driving her away, pushing her further into a life that would destroy her? Maybe we could work this out. Maybe she wouldn't choose to leave home. Maybe . . .*

I hoped for some evidence of remorse, knowing how much she loved being with the family. I longed to hear her say she would quit drinking with her friends and never smoke weed again. I wanted her to say she was sorry. Instead she said, "I've already looked at apartments." The words stung like a slap.

That evening, when Amy went out to join her friends, we stood in her bedroom as we had done so many other nights and prayed. There were few words, yet we knew God heard our heart's cry. I would never forget this night. Unable to sleep, I pleaded with God as tears soaked into my pillow. Hands lifted in the darkness, I surrendered Amy to him.

I awoke in the night from a sound sleep, feeling an urgency to pray. I sensed God had something to say to me. After a time of quiet worship, I waited. In the stillness of the living room, he spoke to my heart so clearly. "You have a rebellious daughter. But in her rebellion she does not walk outside the circle of my love."

The words, though not audible, soothed the pain of my breaking heart like salve on an open wound. God was still at work in Amy's life. I didn't know where her path might lead but I had the assurance that God had not forgotten her.

SEVEN

THE PATH OF REBELLION

Sharon

I have been blessed to be able to stay home and pursue my passion to write. Being a freelance writer sounds more exciting than it really is. One has to have the skin of a rhinoceros to withstand rejection letters and dealing with the unreasonable demands of some editors can be disheartening. Facing the constructive criticism of your peers will make you either a bitter or a better writer.

My sanguine personality makes me a people-person. Working in isolation for long periods of time without talking to anyone is a hardship, but discipline is often my biggest problem. I turn on my computer, check my emails, and only respond to those that need immediate attention. When it's time to buckle down and write, I usually make a valiant start, and then remember there's a load of laundry that needs to be done.

On my way to the laundry room, I hear our cat, Sydney, meowing, so I fill her food bowl. Back at my computer, I launch into an opening paragraph only to have the phone ring and hurry to answer it. If I hear a knock on the door I think it could be one of my neighbours who might need to talk. After our conversation, I remember the houseplants haven't been watered for a week. On and on it goes until my writing time is eaten up by other things. It isn't quite that bad, but some days it feels like it.

The only workable solution would be to have my husband lock me in my office with a lunch tray when he leaves for work, and unlock the door when he gets home. I'd probably find a way to escape through a window.

It is, however, thrilling to see your byline on a published story. Nothing is more rewarding than to have someone tell you how a story or poem you've written encouraged and helped them in some way. The real joy comes in using the creativity that God has given me for his honour and glory.

I reminded myself of this as I sat in my office. The blank computer screen mocked me. What could I possibly write? Nothing seemed to make sense. Amy came into the room quietly, trying not to disturb me. "I've been off drugs for three days," she says. "I'm having trouble sleeping."

I longed to reassure her, to tell her God loved her so much, but I didn't want to add another brick to the wall that stood between us. I hugged her and told her I was praying for her. The words sounded like a cliché, but I had never meant anything more. I asked if she wanted to talk. She didn't. I wished I knew how to reach my daughter's heart. *Lord, I need your wisdom.*

The two weeks we'd given her to make a decision about her lifestyle had passed. In that time, she hadn't talked about moving out, other than her comment about looking for an apartment. As we gathered around the table this time, I waited with mixed feelings. Part of me wanted her to stay. *Please, God, couldn't you accomplish your work in her life here?* Part of me knew she had to go. I had to release her to God.

"I'm serious about quitting drugs," she said. "But I'm still using. I only do them with my friends on weekends, but I'm gonna wean myself off." Her actions backed up her words. I heard a determined Amy planning to do things her own way in her own strength. I felt afraid.

"Then you'll have to move out," Bill said. There was no anger in his voice, only deep sadness, but his words gripped my heart like an iron fist. I knew he was right. We had agreed to take this step, but I had to admit I believed it would never come to this. *Would Amy think we were rejecting her? Would she think the same of God?* I wondered.

I remembered the verses in Daniel I'd read earlier that day. Daniel was thrown into the lion's den because he refused to obey the king's edict. Instead, he had opened his window and prayed to the one true God as was his custom to do three times a day.

The king rolled a stone over the mouth of the den and sealed it " . . . *so that Daniel's situation might not be changed.*"[6] Only God could intervene in what seemed like a hopeless situation and infuse it with hope. I began that day to pray for God's intervention in Amy's life 'to change her situation'. I pleaded with God to keep the roaring lions from destroying our daughter. I knew that as he did, it would bring glory to his name and influence the lives of her friends.

I'm always intrigued by the books God brings across my path at just the right time. One such book I read during this time was "Rebel With A Cause", the story of Billy and Ruth Graham's son, Franklin. It gave me courage to believe for my daughter when I read how Franklin rebelled against his parents. The son of evangelist Billy Graham rebelling? I could hardly believe it.

"I was living a sinful life and still wasn't ready to change, but deep down in my gut, I knew I was wrong,"[7] says Franklin. God delivered him from a life of smoking, drinking and fighting, and transformed his life. I could understand the heart-break his parents must have endured. We were heart-broken too.

Amy continued to promise us and her sisters that every time she went out with her friends would be the last time. That promise was getting stale. In the next breath she said she was determined to quit doing drugs but hadn't made a decision about her relationship with God. My heart cried.

We assured her we would never force her into any decision— that was between her and God. Whenever she went out I wanted the last words she heard to be words of love and not condemnation. Did we always do this well? Absolutely not. We often told her we were praying for her and saw the anguished look on her face. How could she choose a life of pain over a life of peace and joy in Christ? *Lord, doesn't she know the road she's on will lead to disappointment and heartache, and so much more? Please, speak to her in ways that will cause her to hear your voice.*

Amy

"You either live here and change what you're doing, or you move out. You can't live this lifestyle here," my dad said with loving authority in his voice.

"But, Dad, I'm not living it here. I've never done drugs or drank in our home or on our property," I protested. I knew that my parents weren't being unreasonable when they gave me this choice. I also knew that I would move out.

To me smoking some weed and having the occasional drink with friends was hardly a complete lifestyle change. It was just good to have some friends again. It helped me forget the other stuff in my life, gave me something else to think about. The thought of my own apartment, my own life with my new friends was exciting for me. After Chris and I broke up, I felt like I needed something else in my life, something to show I was moving forward.

It was one of those things I did before I even thought about it. I suppose in retrospect that's the way I made most of my decisions. Never one to take time and consider the outcome, if I could do it, I would do it! In this case the "it" was a little apartment in downtown Peterborough. I remember going to see it for the first time in February of 2000. Perfect, I thought, it's just perfect! It's a good size, it has a driveway, and there are no holes in the walls. Besides it's the second apartment I've looked at and I'm getting tired of looking!

EIGHT

PRAYING FOR A ROADBLOCK

Sharon

Early in February Amy told us she wanted to get an apartment of her own. This announcement didn't come as a complete surprise, but it shook me. Amy was still making promises to be off drugs by the end of February—"pie crust promises" Mary Poppins called them. "Easily made, easily broken." We would see that pattern repeat itself again and again. I secretly hoped she would stay here where we could watch her progress and know more about her decisions.

A few days later, Amy asked her dad to cosign for an apartment she'd found. We decided that wasn't the best plan. In the end she lost it. She spent Sunday isolated in her room. She may have resented our decision, but she never admitted it.

My prayers often included a plea that Amy wouldn't find anything she could afford, knowing that it would force her to stay at home. Surely this was a good idea. We could seize every opportunity to speak to her about her lifestyle, if she wanted to listen, and attempt to dissuade her from spending so much time with her friends. Even I knew that wouldn't work.

The determination that fueled Amy's life revealed itself when she found another apartment she really liked three days later. We went with her to see it. The room itself was okay, but we noticed that her door was across the hall from the back door of a Sports Bar. I panicked when we found out she would have to park her car two blocks away and walk to her apartment because there was no parking available on site.

Back at the real estate office we waited as she looked over the paperwork. In my desperation I prayed for a roadblock—something, anything to stop this process. I reminded her about the broken door lock. When she mentioned it, the agent promised to have a peephole and a safety lock installed. Amy agreed to take the apartment.

When we left, she and the agent were signing the papers. I wanted to grab the pen out of her hand and pull her out of the office. I couldn't face the thought of her living in that apartment and walking home alone at night. Panic rose like bile in my throat. *God, where is the roadblock?*

All the way home, I prayed for God to intervene, to somehow prevent her from getting this apartment. But how could that happen? She had already signed the papers. Maybe she would reconsider and stay at home where she would be safe. I knew that was an unrealistic dream.

Sydney, our five-year-old tabby, greeted me at the door, meowing to go outside. I remembered the day Michelle brought her home after work. Someone had left this tiny ball of fur outside in a shopping cart at a K-Mart parking lot. At the end of the day, when no one wanted to take her home, Michelle took pity on her.

The kitten came to us trembling with fear and full of fleas. She was small enough to fit perfectly in the palm of my hand.

As I looked at this tiny creature, I saw another of God's object lessons. He, too, holds his children in the palm of his hand, safe and protected. Often, it seems, we choose to jump out of his hand and go our own way, yet we are never out of his sight.

The girls swayed my resolve against keeping the kitten with the promise of taking over her care, feeding and medical expenses. It was an offer I couldn't refuse. I enjoyed her company, especially today. To keep her from wandering across our neighbour's property, we bought a small harness and attached her to a long cord. It gave her the freedom to roam on our yard, and kept her away from the busy road in front of our house. She could enjoy exploring our lawn safe from harm.

I have never heard the audible voice of God, but as I bent to attach the cord to Sydney's collar that day, he spoke to me. I stood up almost expecting to see God standing behind me. His voice was clear. I will never forget his loving rebuke. "You are treating Amy like Sydney. You think by tethering your daughter to your house, you are able to protect her—keep her safe. Do you not know, my child, that I am able to protect her wherever she goes? She is in my hands. You gave her back into my care and keeping when you dedicated her to me. Trust me now with her life."

Tears streamed down my cheeks as God reminded me again of his unfailing love. I would need that reminder many times over the next few years when fears and pain made me question his ways.

Later that day, Amy came home and sat at the kitchen table, sullen, saying nothing. I was eager to warn her of all the dangers the apartment held, but with great effort I kept my mouth closed.

"The parking fees are $35.00 a month. I can't afford that. I didn't get the apartment." Her words were monotone and flat. She went to her room and shut the door hard. It felt like she was shutting me out of her life. "Thank you, Lord," I whispered. "You did provide the roadblock after all. Forgive me for not trusting you."

Perhaps she would decide to stay here after all. My joy was short-lived. By the end of the week, Amy had found another apartment which the landlord offered to rent on a six month lease. This upper level apartment was located in a residential area rather than downtown. She made an appointment to go and see it. I asked Michelle to come with us.

My heart ached when we walked through the large apartment. It was in sad shape, needing both painting and repairs. Mold covered the inside of the refrigerator. The ceilings showed signs of water leakage. The landlord warned her not to use the small balcony outside the living room window. Noting the rotting boards, I understood why. I tried to find something positive to say about her new home—nothing came to mind except that she was getting a lot of room for her money.

While Amy signed the papers with the landlord downstairs, Michelle and I walked through each room, asking God to fill it with his presence and to protect her in this place. We prayed that she would hear his voice here. As we finished praying, I took one more look around the room. *Should I have prayed for another roadblock?* Fears nibbled around the edges of my faith like hungry rodents. *What will happen in this place? How safe will she be here? What if she never comes home again?*

I left that day shaking my head. How could I have faith one moment and give into fear the next? Fear and unbelief go hand in hand. They show a distrust of God's promises. I couldn't count the times God had proved himself faithful in our lives. How could I ever doubt him? I felt like the man who said to Jesus, "I do believe; help me overcome my unbelief!"[8] I fell on my knees and prayed the same words.

Journal Entry: February 11, 2001

Oh, how my heart aches for Amy. I woke up at 4 a.m. out of a sound sleep and began a long vigil—praying for Amy's protection until she arrived home at 8 a.m.

Sometimes I felt that Michelle's upcoming June wedding was being pushed into the background as we dealt with Amy's situation. The fun we shared as we worked on the wedding plans gave me a respite from my deepening concerns. Trips to the florist, meetings with the caterer, and evenings spent recalling happier times were often the highlights of my days.

She asked her best friend to be her Maid of Honour and her sisters to be her bridesmaids. When you have two sisters, you don't have to look far for wedding attendants. Four years earlier, Michelle and Amy were bridesmaids in Julie's wedding on an unseasonably warm day in May. The sight of our firstborn daughter coming down the aisle on her father's arm, looking beautiful and elegant, engraved a memory on my heart I would cherish forever.

The girls have always been close. When they were children, we tried our best to teach them to forgive each other and not hold grudges. I passed on to them what my mother told me. "Love each other, and be thankful for your family. Treasure each day you have together because there may come a time when you may live far away from each other." Wise words that rang with truth.

Today as we spent the afternoon helping Michelle at her dress fitting, laughter drifted around us like sweet perfume. My breath caught in my throat as the bride-to-be stepped in front of the full-length mirror, smiling and beautiful. My heart swelled with emotion. Another daughter leaving home.

I pushed aside my anxious thoughts as I caught glimpses of a happier Amy, smiling, eager to help, hugging her sisters. They were concerned about their little sister. It showed on their faces.

NINE

FAKE FREEDOM

Sharon

Amy went out on Friday night even though I had commented on the stormy weather. When Bill arrived home and told me about the blowing snow and whiteouts along the highway, uneasiness crept into my mind.

"Visibility is zero near the restaurant," he said, shaking the snow from his coat.

I knew the spot. The wind whips the snow across an open field and piles it onto the road, hiding icy pavement beneath its mounded white shoulders. Over the years we'd seen many accidents there.

I jumped when the phone rang at 6:30. Hearing Amy's voice set off alarm bells in my head. There had been an accident. She lost control. Her car was in the ditch, but she wasn't injured. My heart had a hard time settling back into its normal rhythm. *Had she reneged on her promise to stay off drugs? Were drugs or alcohol the cause of this accident?* My thoughts were jumbled; my prayers mixed with tears.

Bill and Michelle left immediately, my husband shaking his head and muttering that he'd have to take the truck to pull her out. Several hours later when they returned, I heard the rest of the story. They found her car, half buried in snow, between two telephone poles, the front end badly damaged. The impact of the accident packed snow so solidly under the frame and around her car that it required a tow truck to pull it out of the ditch.

If she had gone off the highway a few yards farther and hit a pole, she could have lost her life. *Lord, you have protected our willful daughter once again.*

"I can't believe it!" Michelle sputtered. "She went over and kicked her car. Said something about missing a party tonight. Has she got any brains at all?"

My husband's face looked like a storm cloud ready to burst. "I've never felt more like throttling her than I did tonight. Where's her brain? I told her I could have been identifying her body in a morgue tonight." With that he left the room.

Amy's whole demeanor screamed, "Don't talk to me. I'm mad." She proudly wore the 'I'm-in-control' attitude like a badge. When she did talk it was only to complain that she would miss the party with her friends. As I looked at her, love and anger battled within me. *Doesn't she understand that God protected her? The accident could have taken her life! How fast was she driving? Why is she so reckless? How could we have raised such an irresponsible daughter?* Later that evening, I heard her grumbling that the accident would delay her move to the apartment. I slammed the door on the anger that threatened to erupt like a volcano, and took a deep breath to calm myself.

"This apartment you're so eager to move into will never really be yours. Most of your friends are still living at home. It will be a place where everyone comes to crash, and you'll have little control over what happens." The words came out more harshly than I intended. I felt the chasm widen between us and wondered if I would ever be able to build a bridge across it to reach my daughter.

"My friends aren't like that," she replied. And with that declaration the conversation was over, except for telling me how much cool stuff people have already given her for the apartment.

I remembered hearing this statement, "There are none so deaf as those who will not hear truth."[9] Amy was living proof of that. I knew my words were falling on deaf ears. *Lord, help me not to shout, I told you so, when she discovers the truth.*

Amy
Journal Entry: February 23, 2001

Well, that was interesting. I went out to Dan's to get some weed for tonight and crashed my car on the way home. I pulled out to pass this stupid slow driver, but I hit some ice and slammed into a snow bank between two telephone poles. I can't believe it, of all the nights for something like this to happen. I want to scream. I'm so mad. Anyway, my baggie of weed that was on the other seat went all over the floor. I picked up what I could, but I couldn't get it all. Since Dad was coming to tow me out, I grabbed a whole bunch of gravel and threw it on the floor of the car. I think it worked; it sorta disguised the little pieces of weed that were left. What a crappy night. I mean all I wanted to do was go to Jim's and get high. So much for that, half of my stash is gone, what a waste.

I feel bad that Dad and Michelle had to come and get me. I just keep lying to them, but what else can I do? If I tell the truth there's no way I'll be able to do what I do. Maybe it's better that they don't know, if they did it would just upset them anyway. If they don't know they can't get mad, and if they can't get mad, nothing has to change.

So now, I'm at home waiting for Jim to pick me up so I can still go to the party. I'm so glad he's coming. I really don't want to stay home tonight. Mom and Dad are not happy with me!

Sharon

I remember March 1, 2001 as a sad day. It was several days before my birthday and the reality of Amy moving into her apartment crashed against the hope that this day would never come. Our prodigal daughter has gradually moved farther away from the family in more ways than one.

We helped Amy pack all her belongings into our two vehicles and headed for her new residence. A small spark of hope flickered when we arrived and found the landlord hadn't done the painting or repairs he promised to do. *Will she decide that home is a much nicer place to live?* I wondered.

The state of disrepair didn't bother Amy. Freedom shone too brightly. Michelle and I started cleaning. If she wanted to live here, we'd do what we could to make it smell better. I refused to touch the refrigerator full of mold, insisting she ask the landlord for a new one. *The filthy toilet can stay as it is, I thought. If she wants to have a place of her own, she can clean her own toilet.*

Bill installed a smoke alarm, fixed the door so it actually closed, and put on a safety chain and dead bolt. The pained look on his face reflected his mood. His blood pressure had become a concern over the last few months. Having to leave our youngest daughter in such a place would certainly exacerbate his condition.

Odds and ends of furniture gave the place an eclectic garage sale look. Friends dropped in to see the new digs. "It'll be a good place to crash," I heard them say. I kept my lips tightly pressed together so as not to scream, "I told you so!"

With every load of Amy's things we carried in, I prayed for God's intervention. *Maybe something will go wrong with the rental agreement, and she'll come home, I thought. How could she ever see this place as home? What is driving her to come to this apartment? What will happen here?* All questions for which I had no answers.

I believed that on her own Amy would be faced with the reality of her life. Sometimes being too close to family can be a crutch—depending on them to be your conscience, to make your decisions for you. Now, all the decisions are in her hands, as are all of the consequences. There would be no one looking over her shoulder.

Someone has said, "Choose to sin. Choose to suffer." Sin brags and boasts of the pleasures of a self-indulgent life, but the book of Proverbs gives a clear picture of the truth. Satan's lies are arsenic tablets coated with honey.

As I prayed, God reminded me of the many promises he'd given us, and I recalled the day Michelle and I prayed in this apartment for Amy's salvation and safety. Now we placed her in God's hands once again—where she has been all of her life—and asked that he speak to her as only he can. I felt his sweet peace flood my heart—banishing all my worries and questions. God loves my daughter with a perfect and unfailing love; I can trust him with her life.

When I awoke the next morning, a feeling of sadness surrounded me like a smothering fog. I called Amy to make sure she got up in time for work—something I won't make a habit of doing. I'll miss our chats—we had a lot of those—often talking around one subject until we had thoroughly exhausted all the views. We both found it challenging, though others in the family saw it as distracting, especially when we were watching a movie together.

I found myself expecting to hear her music playing, expecting her to walk into the room, listening for her car in the driveway at dinner time. I felt the separation keenly.

You've lost. I've got her now. She'll never come home. She's turned her back on God and on you. She's mine, I heard the father of lies whispering in my ear.

The following day, I arrived home to find Amy in the kitchen fixing a snack and doing her laundry. I felt a sudden surge of hope. Maybe she was lonely at the apartment. Then I heard her on the phone, talking to a friend and making plans. I quietly reminded myself, she's in God's hands.

Amy dropped in frequently over the next few weeks, usually with a load of laundry. It surprised her to find that her bedroom downstairs had been turned into a workshop and a craft room. We used to laugh together at the television commercial that showed a son heading off to college. Before he was out of the driveway, his parents were measuring his room for the installation of a hot tub.

Amy would have been delighted to find a hot tub in her old bedroom. Maybe that was the way to get her to come back home. I'm sure it would fall under "making the nest more comfortable for the chick."

Amy didn't say much. Maybe that commercial didn't seem so funny any more. I assured her that she could come home any time, and we would welcome her with open arms. What we would not do is try to convince her against her will. God had reminded me many times to love her with an unconditional love. I wasn't always sure what that looked like but everything in me wanted to try. I knew I could only succeed with God's help.

On Sunday, Amy arrived after we got home from church. She admitted she misses being with the family. I secretly hoped she would come to church with us that evening, but I knew I was getting ahead of God. He has a lot to teach our daughter. I hoped she would be willing to learn. We prayed for her every day, asking God to reveal himself to her and lead her to repentance. I could hardly wait for that day to come!

TEN

LETTING GO

Sharon

The longer I live, the more I am able to recognize the many seasons of my life. Life's seasons, like gardening seasons, each offer their own unique beauty. Spring is a season of hope, bringing the anticipation of new growth and new beginnings. It will always be one of my favourite seasons.

I am absorbed in starting seeds, repotting seedlings, and finally planting them out in the flower beds. Weather conditions become my main topic of conversation for anyone who will listen. Despite the threat of frost, I start my seeds outside as early as possible. Seeds germinating in this way are much stronger and do not need to go through the hardening off process which involves putting them outside every day and bringing them in each night to prevent them from being nipped by frost.

My husband has helped me create various ways of covering the seedlings while still keeping them accessible for watering. I'm sure he grows weary of all the garden talk, but he's very helpful when I have a project in mind. The conversation always starts out, "Do you think we could do this? Fix this? Build that?" What I really mean is, "Would you do it for me?"

Summer is a rewarding season. I immerse myself in the continual care of blooming plants and vines, creating alcoves of greenery and spots of beauty. The view from my porch swing is rewarding as I survey my small bit of Eden, peaceful and flourishing. The textures, shapes, colours and fragrances of nature are stunningly beautiful. How creative is our God.

Though I love the sights and smells of the autumn season, I'm never ready to let the flowers go after investing so much time and energy into them. At the first threat of frost, I am outside covering plants, bushes and vines, trying to prolong the blooms as long as possible. My time is spent cleaning up gardens, planting bulbs for a dazzling colour show next year, enjoying the cooler weather, and watching the birds as they make preparations of their own. Autumn is a time of reflection.

In winter, the bulbs, fallen seeds and perennial plants lie dormant in the frozen ground. To the eye, the garden appears dead. Mounds of snow and ice form a comforter for the garden beds, as they wait to be awakened by spring rains. Winter is a time of waiting and rest.

It still amazes me to see the thin pointed tip of a curled tulip leaf push through the hard ground and unfurl before the sun as the seasons change and the earth warms. Plants that were mere dried sticks weeks ago suddenly burst forth in bloom.

I began to realize that God was walking me through the autumn season as we dealt with Amy—a season of letting go. The Master Gardener makes use of every experience in the seasons of our life to produce growth and maturity. Like my gardens, my life needed a lot of weeding and pruning.

Far too often my confidence settled in the things I could do, forgetting that without Christ, I can do nothing at all. Letting go can be a painful process if we try to hold on to things or people God has told us to leave in his care. Our attempts to hold on get in the way of his plans, and cause us grief in the end. It's all about trust. Do we really trust God with everything? Do we trust him with our kids?

We, as mothers, carry these precious gifts from God in our wombs for nine months. During that time we come to know these unborn children as our bodies change in small ways and they grow and move within us, assuring us of new life. When they leave the protection of our wombs through birth, the first sight of their sweet faces brings such inexpressible joy.

God entrusts them into our care and keeping—sometimes for our whole lifetime, and other times for only a few years. We invest vast amounts of energy, time and money in keeping these precious little ones safe from all the dangers of this world. We often come to believe that we are able to do just that—keep them safe all by ourselves, when in reality it is God who watches over them day and night and holds them in the palm of his mighty hand.

God called Abraham to take his son, Isaac, to Mount Moriah. It was the greatest test of trust a father could ever face. In total obedience to God, Abraham was willing to sacrifice his son. When God intervened, providing a ram for the sacrifice, father and son walked back down the mountain together. There is a powerful lesson for all parents in this story. Do we trust God that much? Will we give him our children without question?

Journal Entry: April 27, 2001

"During my time of prayer this morning, the Lord brought this verse to my mind concerning Amy. "And I will restore to you the years that the locust hath eaten . . . "[10] What a promise! One of the meanings of "restore" is to give back something that was lost or taken away.

Wandering in a lifestyle of her own choosing, Amy is lost. As the enemy gradually entices her farther and farther away from Truth, he lays his trap, hoping to snatch away her faith, her dignity, and her life, if he can.

Last night, I had a dream. Amy was standing at the front of our church, praising God with her hands raised. God gave me a strong assurance that it would indeed come true. Even upon waking, I felt the impact of that assurance in my heart though I did not know the time frame. Would I live to see it, or would this happen sometime in the future?

I received no answer to this pressing question except to trust. It seemed strange to me, since Amy doesn't like to be the center of attention, and I couldn't see her going to the front even when she came back to God. She would be more likely to bow her head and quietly commit her life to Christ where she was seated.

I looked up the verse in Joel 2:25 and continued to read. These words brought tears to my eyes. " . . . I will pour out my spirit upon all flesh; and your sons and your daughters shall prophesy, your old men shall dream dreams, your young men shall see visions."[11]

ELEVEN

OUT OF CONTROL

Sharon

The forsythia bush in our front yard, crowned with yellow, bell-shaped blooms, heralded the arrival of May. In the woods across the road, pristine trilliums bloomed in profusion beneath the trees.

My gardener's heart leapt at the sight of multicoloured tulips, yellow daffodils, white narcissus and purple grape hyacinths adorning my garden. Pink bleeding hearts and primroses lined the walkway and masses of pink and purple creeping phlox provided bright splashes of colour.

Sitting in church on a warm Sunday morning, my heart was lifted heavenward as the worship leader invited us to join in songs of praise to the King of Kings. Tears streamed down my cheeks in the awesome presence of God. I prayed for my daughter, asking God to speak to her clearly about her soul, to rescue her from the miry pit of her life.

I had come to church feeling exhausted after a night of little sleep. Every few hours I woke up, heart pounding. I raised my hands in the darkness and prayed for Amy's safety, whispering fervent pleas to my heavenly Father, my words salted with tears. Would I hear a knock on our door one day and open it to find a police officer standing there waiting to tell me they'd found our daughter's body in her apartment, dead of a drug overdose?

As the chorus ended and we were seated, I felt an unexplained intense longing and turned in my seat to look across the congregation. To my surprise I saw Amy sitting beside our daughter Julie and her husband.

I could hardly believe my eyes. Amy in church? My mind shifted into gear as I imagined all the reasons that might have brought her here. Was this the Sunday she would walk into the welcoming embrace of God? I could hardly keep from running to her, enfolding her in my arms and telling her how much Jesus loved her just as she was. For years George Beverly Shea sang the words of an old hymn "Just as I am, without one plea"[12] as Billy Graham invited people to come to forward and accept Christ. This morning I prayed that my daughter would hear that invitation and come to the alter.

When I looked for her after the service, she was gone. I didn't get a chance to speak to her, to tell her how it thrilled me to see her. Disappointment pushed hope aside. After the verse I'd read about God restoring the years the locust had eaten, and the vivid dream, I was sure this was the Sunday our daughter would repent.

I was wrong. This lost sheep would feed on more toxic weeds and drink deeply from more stagnant water holes in a desperate attempt to quench her hunger and thirst. She would walk to the edge of more jagged cliffs and fall into more dangerous pits while she wandered in the enemy's wastelands and continued to run from her heavenly Father.

The question haunted me. Why did she come to church? A few days later, when I mentioned I'd seen her in the service, she told me she woke up hearing church bells ringing after what she described as a horrible night—the worst night of her life. She had come to church that Sunday for reasons she could not fully explain to us.

Amy

I had taken so much that night, so much of everything. It started at a BBQ at a friend's house. A few beers, some joints and before I knew it, it was the worst night of my life.

"Want some?" he asked, holding out his hand so I could see five little pills of ecstasy. "I figured it's the least I could do since you gave me a ride over here."

"Thanks." I quickly grabbed three and popped them down.

"Whoa . . . I uh . . . meant . . . " but before he could finish they were gone.

"Oh, sorry, Rob. I guess I misunderstood," I said as innocently as possible, and smiled sweetly.

"Yeah, no worries. Want a beer?"

"Sure," I said.

As he went into the house, I thought to myself, *if the night keeps going like this I won't have to use any of my stash. It doesn't get much better than this.* Hours went by as we played drinking games and rolled joints. Somewhere a phone rang.

"Hey, Jon is having a house party. Wanna go?"

"I'm in," I said. I had no idea who Jon was, but my X was starting to kick in making the BBQ the most boring place to be. I needed more people and more music.

Heading to the car, Carrie grabbed my arm. "I've got some coke. You in?"

"Hell yes," I replied. We cut a few rails off the coffee table and headed out.

When we got to Jon's little downtown apartment, it was packed with people. All the lights were off, and the whole place was covered in glow-in-the-dark paint. Black lights lit up the crazy squiggly designs on the walls and ceiling. The music pounded as an old streetlight in the corner flashed. It was sensory overload for me. I loved it!

As we danced, it seemed like the whole room was alive. The walls moved with the music. Carrie looked up and pointed at the ceiling.

"Wow. That is so aweso . . . " Before she could finish her sentence she lost her balance and fell over. I saw her on the floor smiling, and burst out laughing. We laughed so hard we were crying.

"I need a drink," I said as I grabbed my sides. Walking into the kitchen, I opened the fridge.

"Yum, Rye."

"Help yourself if you want some," Jon said coming up behind me.

"Great party."

"It could get better. Come with me."

I followed him through the black light maze and into the bathroom.

"You do special K?" he asked.

I smiled and winked. "Only if you're offering." As we snorted a few rails someone pounded on the door.

"If you don't open this door man, I'm gonna puke all over the carpet."

Jon leapt up and unlocked the door. We both ran out as the white-faced guy crawled in.

"Amy . . . Amy . . . " I heard Carrie yelling. I pushed my way through the pie-eyed, sweaty people and found her.

"Hey, Rob and I are leaving. I wanna go see Jason tonight."

I looked at my watch. It was three a.m. "Sure, I'm in."

As we got in the car, my head started to spin. I fixed my eyes on the seat in front of me and tried to slow my breathing. My teeth were clenched so tight I could only breathe through my nose. Sweat poured off me. I desperately tried to act calm. I didn't want anyone to know what was going on. After all, I was the girl who could do anything, who could handle anything. I was invincible.

Rob pulled up to the curb and we all piled out.

"I'm gonna go park. Don't drink my beer," he said as he drove away.

I tried to concentrate on every step as I climbed the stairs to Jason's apartment. I calculated every movement of my legs and feet, and somehow stayed upright. I knew if I didn't rest for a while I would pass out. My heart felt like it would pound out of my chest.

When I got in I mixed a strong Rye and Coke and went into the bathroom. I downed the drink, and locked the door. The bathroom floor felt cold against my back. I was drenched in sweat, my breathing shallow and quick. My eyes closed and the room began to spin.

Okay, just a minute more, I thought to myself. Slowing my breathing, I opened my eyes, got up and looked in the mirror. *Hold it together. Hold it together.* The moment began to pass. I opened the door and walked into the living room.

"There she is. Amy can do it. Seriously, I've seen it," someone said.

"What's up?" I asked.

"151 proof? She says you can take a full shot of it," Jason said as he filled the shot glass.

"Depends. Is there money on the table?"

"Well there's a hit of X in it for you if you do two in a row," Jason replied.

"Two in a row," Carrie yelled. "That's just mean!"

"Fill it up," I said with a smile. *Mind over matter*, I thought. *Mind over matter*. Grabbing one shot in each hand I quickly downed the left, then the right. My throat felt like it was raw and bleeding.

"Where's my prize?" I asked.

Jason stood up and took his hat off. "I'm impressed," he said, handing me the small round pill.

"Thanks," I smiled, thinking I was going to puke. "On that note, we should go."

"Amy, are you getting a cab? Do you need a ride? I can take you home," Jason offered.

"Sure, that saves cab money. Thanks."

As I climbed into the car the thought occurred to me. *Who is this guy? I don't even know him*. We pulled up to my apartment. As I got out, Jason asked, "Can I use the bathroom?"

'Yeah, okay."

As soon as I opened the door, Jason headed for the bathroom. I flopped on the couch. As I lay there I started to hyperventilate again. My arms became weak, and my heart raced.

I felt something heavy on me--something touching my face. Kissing. Someone was kissing me. I opened my eyes.

"What are you doing? No! Get off . . . you can't . . . ." My words were mumbled and slow. I moved my arms trying to push him off, but he grabbed my wrists and held them. I realized I was too weak to fight back. My body had finally given out. I tried to speak, tried to yell, tried to kick and punch and scratch, but I had no strength left. I kept fading in and out.

When I finally came to, my eyes slowly opened. My body hurt. I started to remember what happened. Hot tears poured down my face. I curled up into a ball and pulled all the blankets over my naked body. Through my sobs, I wondered, *Why? How? What am I doing?* I couldn't gain control. I couldn't stop crying.

Faintly, in the distance, I heard something I'd never heard before in my apartment. Church bells. I stopped crying and listened. The bells rang out loud and clear. Where they came from I didn't know. I'd never heard them before or since that morning.

As I lay there listening, something began to calm me, to comfort me. I sat up as a single thought filled my mind. *It's Sunday. I should go to church.*

TWELVE

WEARING MASKS

Sharon

One Sunday after church, Bill's mother took us out for dinner to celebrate our 30th anniversary. We arrived home just in time to pick up the phone before the answering machine took the message.

Bill put down the receiver, shaking his head in disbelief.

"Amy's been in a car accident," he said. My stomach twisted into knots. "It happened Friday night. It was raining hard and she rear ended the driver in front of her when he slowed down for a pot hole in the road. She probably wrote off her car. And why are we hearing about it two days later?" Anger edged his voice. "Why didn't she let us know the night it happened?"

When she came home a few days later, we heard more details. She was charged with careless driving, incurred a fine and lost six demerit points. She told us someone had given her a drink earlier, but she didn't drink it. When the police officer asked if she'd been drinking, she answered "no". Our daughter, who is no stranger to alcohol, said she chose not to drink that

71

night. I prayed it was true but I feared she couldn't distinguish the truth from lies any more.

She sat at the kitchen table, her face a mask of conflicting emotions.

"What's wrong?" I said.

"You didn't even bother to ask if I was hurt when I told you about the accident." I could hear the little girl hidden beneath her tough exterior crying for someone to care. Her accusing words tore at my heart like talons. Did she know how much pain they inflicted? How could she believe we didn't care about her?

"You're giving off signals that clearly tell us you don't want us involved in your life, that you can handle everything yourself," I replied, swallowing my pain and trying to keep the frustration out of my voice. "I'm sorry, Amy, I guess we assumed that since you didn't say you were hurt, you were okay." Her eyes said more, but she didn't speak.

I went with her to clean out her car. The guy who towed it told us it was a write-off. Looking at the twisted metal I thanked God she was safe. I helped her fill two large garbage bags with armloads of fast food wrappers, coffee cups and cigarette packages from the back seat, and all the junk stuffed into her trunk. I wondered how we got to this place. Where had we gone wrong as parents?

For a moment I was overwhelmed by the need to fix this mess—to rush in and do something to make everything right again, to go back to happier days. As I stood beside Amy, I realized that I couldn't change anything about her life any more than I could fix her wrecked car. I could only pray!

Tears stung my eyes. What will it take for Amy to release control of her life to the God who loves her so perfectly? She has pulled the cloak of "I-can-handle-everything- myself" more tightly around her, clearly indicating she's not ready to relinquish control today. Standing beside her mangled car, I prayed God's protection over our unruly daughter for what seemed like the hundredth time, fearing that this cloak might one day become a shroud.

The brunt of the financial implications cut deeper worry lines into my dear husband's face. Amy was on his insurance policy, so our rates will soar. I saw the signs of stress in his eyes and his slouched shoulders. This accident added more weight to the load he was carrying, not just financially but physically and emotionally.

Recently, he told me that God spoke to him, reprimanding him for turning the guest room into a place to have a pity party. This room was his prayer closet—dedicated as a place to pray for his daughters. Lately, instead of praying for them, and especially for Amy, he had begun to complain about the things that were happening. Doubt crept in, and he wondered if Amy would ever come back to the Lord. After that experience with God, his prayers changed. He resolved to trust God completely with her life.

Often I woke up and I found his side of the bed empty and knew that he was on his knees praying. He spent many hours behind that closed door, the same one I used to tentatively push open so many nights to see if Amy had come home. I am thankful for his willingness to listen and obey God. My husband is a blessing to my life.

Plans for Michelle's June wedding and Dad's 75th birthday celebration kept us busy and brought a sense of reprieve to the stress. My dad, Herman, is a godly man, steadfast in his faith. Though a humble man of few words, his compassion and his servant's heart are evident for all to see. I called him many times asking him to pray for Amy. The wisdom that flows from his love for God, soothed my hurting soul like a healing ointment.

The shopping, bridal showers and checking of endless details have given me something else to think about and have kept us in a whirlwind of activity. With Julie and Amy in the wedding party, the whole family was working hard to make Michelle's wedding day as perfect as possible. It helped immensely that she has an easy-going personality and doesn't let the normal glitches and problems of planning a wedding distress her.

On the day of the wedding, I awoke early to see blue sky peeking through the clouds. The house was quiet. The songs of birds mingled with my prayers of thanksgiving. Soon the stillness gave way to an explosion of activity. A sense of peace enveloped me as I watched as the photographer take pictures of Michelle running though a field with her veil blowing in the breeze. Our sweet Michelle will be united in marriage to a man who loves God and will love and care for her.

She and Craig have known each other all of their lives. They grew up in Calvary Church together. We found a picture of them when they were kids in their Crusader uniforms which made them laugh. They remembered the days when their dads were on the church baseball team together and they played on the swings and climbers in the park during the games. Craig recalled that at one of those games, when they were about five years old, he told Michelle he would marry her someday.

After a beautiful wedding and reception, family and friends gathered at our home to share some time with the newly-weds as they opened a few gifts. As is our tradition, we showered them with confetti and sent them off with our congratulations. I glanced at Amy and wondered what thoughts were going through her mind.

Before they left on their honeymoon, Michelle surprised us with a unique gift. Inside a carved wooden box we found these simple instructions: Each of you is to open one card a day.

When everyone had gone, Bill and I sat in the confetti-strewn room reminiscing. Our second daughter was married and would begin a new life with her husband. I knew she would still come home, but it wouldn't ever be the same. When I passed her door on the way to bed, I peeked in to see an empty room. A lump rose in my throat. *Thank you, Lord, for your faithfulness. You watched over Michelle and Craig and brought them together in your time.*

We will open one card each day from Michelle's Memory Box—her gift to us. It amazes me how God uses every day things to encourage and remind us of his loving care.

The first one Bill opened brought a smile to his face. It read: "Dad, there is nobody I am more proud of than you. You are the best role model I could ever have asked for. I love you."

Several days later he read this one: "Dad, thank you for teaching me the importance of tithing. I looked for those little white envelopes every Sunday, and I was never disappointed. Your example still guides me today."

My cards were equally touching. "Mom, I'll never forget the morning prayers you had with us, as kids, when we were leaving for school. I understand now, though I didn't at the time, just how important they were." Another one said, "Mom, thank you for teaching me simple courtesies and respect. Treating people how you want to be treated, and serving them with an open heart."

The card we chose today read: "I want to thank you both for your unconditional love shown to me through every situation, every trial and every celebration. Both of you has been the best example, throughout my life, of God's unconditional love.

There is no greater comfort to me than this: wherever I go, whatever I do, I will always be loved by God, and I will always be loved by both of you."

I believe God arranges moments like these to encourage parents not to give up when things get tough and they don't see an end to the struggles they are going through.

The words were like a warm hug. Even with all our faults and dismal failures, our children have managed to catch glimpses of Christ in us. Our family members are the ones who see us up close and personal every day. Our kids take note of our attitudes and actions, watching to see whether or not they line up with what we say. We can put on a good front for others, but we can't fool those who live with us for very long. They watch to see if we are 'walking-the-talk'.

We will always treasure these memories from Michelle's heart.

THIRTEEN

CONFESSION

Sharon
Journal Entry: August 1, 2001

My Scripture reading this morning brought me to the story of Samson. The words " . . . *and the Spirit of the LORD began to stir him . . .* "[13] caught my attention. Samson was a young man who experienced the presence of God throughout his life and performed great feats of strength. His self-indulgent life left him bound and blind. In the end, humbled and shamed, he called on God one last time.

The words became my prayer for Amy. "Stir her heart, Father, as only you can. Holy Spirit, pursue her as the Hound of Heaven. Touch and soften her hardened heart with your love. Take away her appetite for drugs and the music she listens to. Change her desire for the decaying scraps the world offers to a hunger for the rich feast you provide."

One day, Amy called and asked the family to come over to her apartment. This was a first. A hundred thoughts rushed through my mind. *What's this about? Had something terrible happened? Was she sick of her life? Had she decided to come home?* My heart leapt at that thought.

I felt a tremor of fear as we were seated. Amy sat apart from us on a windowsill, smoking. My stomach fluttered as I waited to hear what she had to say. It wasn't what I expected at all. She told us she was still using drugs until a few weeks ago, and apologized for lying to us.

"I really want to kick the habit," she said. "I love the high, but I have to do more and more to get the thrill. I want to move away—away from all my friends—make a clean start."

She went on to tell us that she was high the Sunday she came to church. She had come to the only place she knew she could get help. The guilt and shame she felt over hurting her family, the ones who loved her most, weighed heavily on her. Even as she told us, the pain was written all over her face.

As we hugged her and prayed for God to continue his work in her life, I recalled my recent prayer. "*God, please take away her appetite for drugs and the music she listens to.*" Tonight, God graciously showed me that he is always at work in those we pray for even when we don't see anything happening.

Her confession to us marked a big step forward and an affront to the enemy's powerful hold over her. I knew we must pray more fervently for Amy. The enemy can't win the battle for her soul. One of my life verses is found in Isaiah 59:19: " . . . When the enemy shall come in like a flood, the Spirit of the LORD shall lift up a standard against him."[14]

In Bible times, when an army went into battle, they raised a standard or a flag in front of the soldiers. As long as the standard was elevated, the soldiers continued to fight. It's reassuring to know that it is God who raises the standard against the enemy for us. He also promises to be our forward and rear guard. We are protected on all sides against the enemy of our soul as long as we place our confidence and trust in the God of our salvation.

It reminded me of a time when I thought I could stand against an actual flood in my own strength. In rainy weather the lower end of the field behind our property sometimes becomes a catch basin for all the run off. Eventually a large pond forms, filling with more and more water until it suddenly gives way.

That day as I stood watching, it burst like a weak dam, sending a deluge of brown water across our yard. I snatched up a piece of plywood and held it against my legs, hoping to prevent the flood from gouging out our driveway. The force of the water nearly knocked me off my feet. It twisted the wooden shield out of my hand and swept it away, leaving a trail of uprooted plants in its wake.

It was a picture of what the enemy will to do in our lives if we attempt to stop him ourselves, without standing under the protection of God's standard. I knew the father of lies would try every tactic to drown Amy in a flood of shame and guilt, urging her to believe that she was worthless and unloved, and convincing her that she had sinned too much to come back to God.

When God inspired me to write a poem about the prodigal son from the father's perspective, I thought of my own rebellious daughter. I read the story again and saw her in every line.

My heart ached for Amy to understand God's father heart toward her.

A few days later, I drove to the retail store where she worked and placed the poem on the front seat of her car with a note that said: "Your heavenly Father loves you more than you can imagine. Dad and I love you and we will never stop praying for you."

HEART PAINS

She's gone.
Packed her things,
Waved goodbye and left,
To live a different life, she said
 In a place of her own
Far away from home.

Each pink-streaked dawn
The father's work-worn hands
Fling wide the door.
Stiffened legs are pressed to run.
Sleep-filled eyes strain to see
If she is coming home.

Twilight's creeping hours mark his lonely vigil,
Patiently waiting, praying, searching the dim
Horizon for a glimpse of his dear one.
And when the inky night blots out the road
A candle flickers in the dark
To light his daughter's way home.

CONFESSION

Through summer's shimmering heat
The father toils on. A thousand times
He wipes his weary eyes
And gazes at the empty road,
Heart lurching at the slightest sound
Hoping to see his loved one coming home.

In the midst of harvest feasting
He leaves the music, leaves the celebration
Far behind. He hungers not for food
But for the sight of one he loves.
How can every smiling face
Remind him of his daughter?

Tender longing draws his eyes to
The leaf-strewn road royally bedecked
With a carpet of crimson and gold,
As if the trees themselves had
Made extravagant preparation
Ready to welcome her home.

Endless gray days wrap him in sadness
Like a season of mourning.
Shoulders hunched against the cold,
His tears freeze on his cheeks.
Does she have a warm coat?
He would gladly give her his.

The frost-encrusted path between
Black skeletal trees shows no sign of
Life as far as the eye can see.
His only scarf adorns the gate
Lest in the blinding snow
She should lose her way.

Freed from winter's icy grip
The earth discards her sodden coat
And dons a robe of green.
The father walks the fields and prays.
Upon the highest hill he waits,
Facing the rising sun.

In the swirling mist upon the road
The father fixes his gaze upon
A distant shadow moving alone.
Heart pounding, he shades his eyes
To see if it might be his daughter
Making her way home.

With eyes downcast and shoulders bent
The figure moves with limping step.
Each stone and tree along the way
Shouts memories of another day
When she was small and loved to be
Cradled upon her father's knee.

In the field the father cries
Tears of joy, tears of pride.
His plodding feet unfettered now

Run and skip and leap and twirl.
Arms reaching,
Heart bursting,
Laughing
Waving
Calling.

His daughter is coming home.

Amy
Journal Entry: August 22, 2001

Mom left a poem in my car today at work. It was about the prodigal returning. I cried so hard when I read it. I know it's true, I know that this isn't what I was meant for. This life isn't what anyone is meant for. I thought this life would be cool. But now I'm starting to realize there's nothing worthwhile or lasting about it. It's stripped me of everything, my morals, values, self-worth and identity.

Instead of glamour I have ugliness, instead of peace I have sleepless nights, instead of a high I have a constant hunger. Embraces that I thought would share love and meaning are only empty sex. So much for fun and excitement, now I'm just broken.

Part of me wishes I could go back. Back to the truth, back to being honest and real. But there's no way that's going to happen. I can't go a day without a drink or a hit of something. It consumes my thoughts, like a monster that wells up and takes me over. I think I'm in too far to change.

FOURTEEN

LISTENING

Sharon

I looked forward to our next visit expecting to hear Amy's reaction to the poem. I hoped she hadn't thought I was pushing her to make a decision. God knew everything about her, and loved her. We tried to show her that we did too, even though we were hurting over the life she chose to live. We told her our door was always open for her to come home.

When she finally dropped by, she didn't mention the poem. Instead she told me that one of her friends came with her to the nine o'clock service on Sunday. My husband and I served as ushers in the second morning service and had missed seeing them. As she talked, God reminded me that he wanted me to continue to pray for her friends. Sadly, I realized I hadn't prayed for these precious girls at all over the past few years.

A small smile pulled at the corners of her mouth as she told me she's been clean for two weeks. "I'm not having a problem with the physical appetite for drugs," she admits, "but I do miss the high. It's harder to stay clean when I'm alone and bored." She pauses. I wait. "I cry when I'm alone in my apartment."

I pulled her close. She didn't resist. *Crying alone.* Those words thundered in my ears and flashed a heart-wrenching picture in my mind. *Alone? Can't she see that she is never alone? Has she forgotten that God is always with her? Does she understand now that her friends will never be there for her when she needs them?*

I believe she is experiencing God's presence as he exposes the sin in her life and urges her to repent. It's what we've been praying for, day after day, for five years—sometimes with faith in our hearts that it is just around the corner, and sometimes with more doubt than faith when we hear more and more about her life.

The war for her soul was escalating. The heavenly combatants were aligned against the enemy and his minions. Some days I felt the spiritual battle taking place around us. I could almost hear the enemy, laughing, taunting, and boasting of his victory.

She's gone too far to turn back now. I am in control of her life. She'll never leave me!

I couldn't get the picture of her crying alone in her apartment out of my mind. I hated how the enemy continued to deceive her. How I wished she would call me. I would rush over and hold her in my arms, stroke her hair, and pour out all my love on her. Perhaps that was why she didn't call. She still believed the lie that she had control of her life. *What will it take? How much lower will she sink? How much more pain can she bear before she calls out to the Father?*

86

Journal Entry: September 11, 2001

When I woke up this morning I had no idea that on this day the world would change forever. The first news reports provided limited information. An airliner flew into one of the Twin Towers in New York City. The people that I talked to in the grocery store were surprised, and then shocked as we heard a short time later that another plane hit the second Tower.

It seems the whole world is holding its breath. I watched in horror as pictures of buildings collapsing into piles of rubble flashed on the television. Later, we heard reports that al-Qaeda terrorists had hijacked four commercial passenger airlines, intentionally crashing two of them into the World Trade Center, and one into the Pentagon. A fourth plane crashed in a field in Pennsylvania after a courageous attempt by the crew and some of the passengers to take control.

The loss of life was staggering. Reports say almost 3,000 people died. The border between the U.S.A. and Canada is closed, as are the airports. Military security is on high alert. Each new report includes more images of the disaster. The emotional impact is crushing; the load of information overwhelming. I feel numb.

As I sat in my doctor's office this afternoon, nervously waiting to hear test results, I desperately wanted to gather our family together to pray for those who have lost loved ones, for those who are risking their lives to save others. It's time we humbled ourselves as a country before Almighty God and confessed our desperate need of him. I didn't think to pray for the terrorists.

My thoughts turned to Amy. Had she seen the news? Would she be afraid? I wondered if this would cause her to think about her life. Her eternal life. Would this be the moment she runs back to her heavenly Father?

The words from this morning's Scripture reading take on fresh meaning. "He will be *the sure foundation* for your times, a rich store of salvation and wisdom and knowledge; the fear of the LORD is the key to this treasure" (Isaiah 33:6).[15]

You, Lord, are the only sure foundation that will hold firm, even in disastrous times like these.

Spring and fall are my two favourite seasons, probably because they coincide with the beginning and ending of the gardening season. For me, gardening is an absolute passion. I simply cannot keep myself from gardening. No matter how I feel, or what deadlines await, I will inevitably choose to battle the hordes of mosquitoes that call my yard home, and work in my garden. The sign that hangs in my garden says it all: GARDEN: It's where your heart can bloom.

Spring thrills me with its distinctive earthy smell and a serenade of bird songs. Autumn inspires me with flowers at their peak of beauty, and a crispness in the air that hints of winter while still clinging to summer's warmth. The first severe frost that destroys all my tender annuals nearly brings me to tears. These are plants I have nurtured, watered and fertilized over the summer months to produce a beautiful display.

God often speaks to me in my garden, not in an audible voice but by drawing my attention to object lessons that apply to my spiritual growth.

I am a hesitant pruner. I don't enjoy cutting back healthy vines and shrubs to produce a bountiful show of blooms the next year. God prunes the unproductive branches from my life in order to more truly reflect his beauty, his nature and to produce more fruit. His pruning is hard to bear, but the results are always for my benefit and for his glory. I'm learning to submit to The Master Gardener as he patiently does his work in my life.

I've noticed he is teaching me to listen to his voice before I say or do anything. I wish I could say I've learned this lesson, but my actions often reveal that I still have a long way to go. I'm a talker and sometimes my mouth starts speaking before my mind is fully engaged.

When Amy dropped in to do laundry this week, I could see she had something on her mind. She admitted having a hard time staying off drugs. I wanted to jump in and tell her that trying to do it on her own, in her own strength, would never work. I felt restrained, as if God was tapping me on the shoulder and reminding me to listen—really listen to what Amy was saying. I kept quiet.

"I feel like there's a war going on inside me. It's tearing me in two. I just can't take it any more," she said, struggling to hold back the tears.

Choosing to ignore God's directive to listen, I jumped in and reminded her that she was in good company. "The apostle Paul said exactly the same thing," I told her. "The things he wanted to do, he didn't; the things he didn't want to do, he did. And he described it as a war too."[16] I thought my paraphrase would help her to understand.

"I know how to come back to God," she said. "But it would be boring. I'd miss all the fun I have with my friends."

I wanted to scream, *What fun? What friends? You are destroying your life!* Instead I held her hands in mine, looked straight into her eyes and assured her of God's love, and ours. *Was she even listening to these words?* I wondered how long the war would rage inside her before she realized that the peace she was so desperate for could only be found in Jesus Christ.

In my prayer times over the next few days, I found myself thinking of the widow in Luke's gospel. Jesus tells a parable about a persistent widow who comes repeatedly to a judge to plead for justice. I am persisting too. I come pleading for Amy's salvation.

Fragments of a song I'd heard drifted into my thoughts like a refreshing stream. *Some are calling you a prodigal. Some aren't calling you at all. But far away someone is calling you back home. Do you hear it anymore out there on your own.*[17] The words brought a fresh flow of tears and a loving reminder— God was still calling Amy home.

Sometimes she seemed so close to leaving her sinful life behind and reaching out to a new life in Christ. Other times I thought, *she's a million miles away.* On days when my faith faltered and I didn't know what else to do, I prayed. "Lord, I am encouraged by the truth that even though my prayers may be repetitious, I am praying your will, Father. You long for everyone to come to repentance through Jesus, your Son."

I'm learning to place Amy in God's hands every day. She is his child. When my faith came in line with this truth, my anxious thoughts disappeared. I remembered the dream I had six months ago of her standing at the front of the church, coming home to her Father, and peace filled my heart. I made a commitment to the Lord: In my thinking and in my words, Lord, it will always be 'when' she comes home, not 'if'.

I think God knew I needed a bit of encouragement. When Amy came home for a quick visit, she told me she'd been praying and asking God for his help. She said she felt happier than she had in a long time. The look on her face confirmed the truth of her words. I encouraged her to keep praying and reminded her that God would never leave her. She seemed reluctant to say more.

One Sunday in late October, Julie and her husband came for lunch after church. It surprised me to see her place a rather large vitamin tablet next to her plate. She has never been able to swallow pills, let alone one that size.

The thought that popped into my mind burst out of my mouth before I had time to think about it.

"Is there a special reason you are taking such a huge vitamin?" One look at the way her face lit up told me the answer.

"We're expecting," she said. I jumped up and hugged her. My husband grinned.

Grandparents. What a wonderful word. I remembered something I had underlined in my Bible years ago when our children were young, something Paul said to Timothy. "I have been reminded of your sincere faith, which first lived in your grandmother Lois . . . "[18]

"Lord," I prayed, "the desire of my heart is that you would help me to have that kind of faith, set that kind of example for my children, my grandchildren, and my great grandchildren."

FIFTEEN

LOVING UNCONDITIONALLY

Sharon

I enjoy reading through the Bible from Genesis to Revelation. Usually I started each morning with a chapter in the Old Testament, followed by one in the New Testament. Have I been consistent? I'd like to say yes, but the truth is there were times I allowed other things to crowd into my time with God. On the days I neglected his Word, things didn't go as well. Seeing my unopened Bible filled me with regret because it meant I'd missed what God wanted to say to me that day as I waited in his presence.

My attitude required an adjustment every morning and my motives needed to come under the scrutiny of the Holy Spirit if I truly desired to be a clear reflection of Christ to those I encountered in my day. And that included my family. They had an upfront and personal view of my life.

Today, I opened my Bible to Psalms, and thumbing through, stopped at Psalm 112 where I had been reading the day before. "Blessed is the man who fears the LORD, who finds great delight in his commands. Even in darkness light dawns for the upright, for the gracious and compassionate and righteous man. He will have no fear of bad news; his heart is steadfast, trusting in the LORD."[19]

The phrase, " . . . no fear of bad news . . . ," started the same old chorus of 'what ifs' in my mind. *What if something terrible happened to Amy in her apartment? What if she drifted farther and farther from God? Would she ever find her way back? What if . . . ?*

One of the enemy's best tactics is to distract us with all the things that *could* happen—few of which ever do. As I read the Psalm again another phrase rose up to momentarily halt the marching 'what if's'. The words, " . . . even in darkness light dawns for the upright . . . ," would become even more meaningful over the next few days even though I felt discouraged because I knew "upright, gracious, compassionate and righteous" were not attributes that described me all of the time. If they were evident, it was only because of God's grace.

A week went by before we had a chance to drop off the coffee table we'd found at a yard sale for Amy's apartment. We didn't make a habit of showing up uninvited. She might think we were checking up on her. God had given me plenty of reminders about loving her unconditionally, rather than telling her how to live her life. I had to come to terms with the idea that loving her unconditionally did not mean condoning her behaviour or decisions. Leaving Amy in his hands meant taking my hands off and trusting God to do his work in her life.

My natural inclination is to sit down and talk about a problem for as long as it takes until we find a solution. God, I've noticed, uses a different approach. It feels like he taps me on the shoulder and turns me around. He gently places his hands on either side of my face, like I used to do when I wanted to have my child's full attention. Then he smiles like a father who has repeated these words a billion times, and says, "I Am the solution to all of your problems. I Am your peace."

What we saw in her apartment when we arrived astounded us. The kitchen looked like a distillery. Piled up against one wall, almost to the ceiling, were empty bottles—whiskey, vodka, rum, tequila—a proud display of riotous living.

My husband turned to leave the room. When I asked him what he was thinking, he told me he told me the sight of those bottles brought back too many painful memories. His father had died an alcoholic and he couldn't bear to think of his own daughter going down the same destructive road.

I stayed in the kitchen still staring at the wall of glass. *Her friends must be heavy drinkers*, I thought. *I knew they'd be a bad influence.* I argued silently in my daughter's defence. *She might be drinking, but not as much as them.* I struggled to believe what I wanted so desperately to be true.

Suddenly the words I had read a few days ago, " . . . no fear of bad news . . . " flooded into my mind. The sight of those bottles had shocked me like the bad news of a sudden death. I had little knowledge of alcoholism, but I knew that binge drinking was the main cause of alcohol poisoning. With Amy's drive to prove herself, I knew she would not stop until she out drank everyone in the room. I didn't let myself dwell on how many of those bottles she had emptied by herself. The answer would crush my hope.

Tears stung my eyes as I stood there in stunned disbelief. Then I felt a keen awareness of God's presence surrounding me. Slowly, like a bud opening before the sun, the words " . . . even in darkness light dawns . . . " pushed aside the pain in my heart and offered hope. Would I seize that truth and believe, or give in to despair? The choice was mine.

I couldn't take my eyes off those bottles. My daughter is an alcoh—even in my mind, I couldn't finish the word. I refused to speak it aloud. Somehow saying it would make it true. Deep inside I knew it was true though I raged against the reality.

In my turmoil, a sinister voice mocked me. *"You are a failure. Everyone will find out and blame you. People are already talking about your family behind your back. Your testimony will be ruined. How could a girl who went to Sunday school and church and read her Bible end up like this unless her parents made serious mistakes? She'll end up dead in a ditch."*

Dead in a ditch. Those words tore at my soul, leaving me in physical pain. *Amy only weighs 115 pounds. She could die of alcohol poisoning.* Examples of my failure as a parent rushed through my mind like a movie on fast forward. *I should have seen the signs,* I berated myself. *What kind of mother doesn't know her daughter is addicted to alcohol? Have I been too lenient with her because she's the youngest? Have I walked through life with my eyes closed, too busy with other things to notice?*

Days later, some of my worst fears would be realized and I would learn how to trust God in the darkest of nights.

SIXTEEN

ANCHORED IN THE STORM

Sharon

As the holiday season approached I tried to forget what I saw in Amy's apartment. Christmas in our house is always an event. I have been called a "Christmas fanatic", and rightly so. I start decorating the house by the first of November. Our artificial tree for the family room is hauled out of storage by the end of November for what we call "tree decorating night"—an event that is marked on the calendar early so everyone can check their schedules.

The whole family shares in the fun—some willingly; some by coercion. Bill and Michelle begin the evening by putting the tree together—branch by branch—to the familiar strains of Christmas carols. Then it's my turn to add the strings of coloured lights and the star. The family has been kind enough to snap unflattering pictures of me putting the star in place while perched precariously on a step ladder. Julie and Amy have the job of draping the garland and hanging most of the ornaments.

The men in the family—my husband and our sons-in-law—are less enthusiastic about this tradition than the women. They participate by adding one ornament to the tree. I think it's the food that keeps them coming back.

When the tree is decorated, the lights in the room are turned off and the Christmas tree lights turned on to the "oohs" and "ahs" of everyone. When the guys have had enough of this Christmas routine, they grab the remote and try to find a hockey game before the girls slip "It's A Wonderful Life" into the DVD player.

I'm sure there are those who don't understand why a family who all live in the same city get so excited about being together. It's hard to explain except to say we are an exceptionally close family and have always enjoyed each other's company.

On the first Saturday in December, as the tantalizing aroma of ginger cookies wafted through the house and Christmas carols were playing, I reminded my husband that it was time to put up the real tree.

Bill and I donned our warmest clothes and started the hunt for the perfect Christmas tree. We prefer a Balsam Fir—just the right height and width. The search took us to several locations where we checked out the trees for height, shape, and freshness.

Today, the cold hurried our choice. One good thump of the trunk on the ground to check for falling needles settled the matter. Bill loaded the tree into his truck and off we went. Often this ritual has been carried out in bitterly cold, windy weather. All for the love of a fresh Christmas tree.

Within moments of securing it in the tree stand, the room was filled with its intoxicating fragrance. It has become a custom to leave the live tree up as long as possible. It started when I decided to extend our Christmas celebration to honour my Ukrainian heritage. Ukrainian Christmas festivities begin on Christmas Eve and end on the Feast of the Epiphany, usually the sixth of January. By that time the tree had been up about five weeks, but I noticed that it was still fresh and green. Each year I left it up a little longer, keeping it well-watered.

One year, I was surprised to find new pale green growth at the ends of several branches. How could I discard a living, flourishing tree. So day by day the tree's life was extended. Now I take it down between the middle and the end of February. I love the Christmas season.

I have a collection of manger scenes, but my favorite is the one that fills the space in front of our living room window. My husband constructed a crude wooden manger which is filled with hay. A life-like doll wrapped in a soft white cloth represents baby Jesus and a menagerie of woolly sheep are gathered around the manger.

Family, friends and neighbours who frequent our home during this festive season have commented on the display, some asking questions, some drawn to the baby, and some reaching back into their past to recall Christmases of their own. The children like to lift the baby from the manger and place the doll among the sheep, creating their own version of the manger scene. The Good Shepherd with his sheep—it works.

This Christmas season, I was keenly aware of our lost sheep. She seemed quiet, more withdrawn and detached than she had been over the last few months. Something was terribly wrong. I could feel it, see it in her eyes. *What was it?*

Several days after our family tree decorating night, she stopped by after work, looking pale and tired. "Are you sick?" I asked.

"I've been throwing up for the past two days. Probably the flu."

She managed to keep down some homemade chicken soup, toast, and ginger ale. We laughed about ginger ale having medicinal properties. Perhaps she was comparing it to the contents of the bottles in her apartment. While she napped on the couch, I prayed that God would speak to her through what she saw and heard this Christmas season.

The next day she called to say she'd gone to the Emergency Ward, and was diagnosed with a stomach virus. The doctor said she was dehydrated and should take it easy over the next few days. My mind leapt to the thought that this was somehow alcohol related.

When she phoned the following day, I knew she wanted to talk. "I'm back to work, Mom. And I've quit smoking." I heard the pride in her voice. "I'm not seeing my friends as much, but it's really hard being alone." She went on to tell me how lonely it was not having any other friends to turn to, and how thankful she was for her family.

"I'll be home for my birthday, and for all of the Christmas holiday." The excitement in her voice was unmistakable. I believed God was working in her heart, but kept that thought to myself. I didn't want her to think I was trying to manipulate her feelings. I didn't want her to change her mind about coming home.

In my reading this morning, I found comfort in this verse in Isaiah. " . . . those who hope in the LORD will renew their strength."[20] What would I do without God's Word? It was my anchor as we rode out this storm. When the waves threatened to sink us, and the thunder crashed around us, and the lightning strikes were so close we felt the electricity in the air, having Jesus in the boat with us made all the difference.

I'm trying to be strong. It only works when I'm leaning on God. In my own strength, I would fall flat on my face. Not a bad position to be in before the God of all creation. The waiting part was hard. I preferred action. Waiting seemed useless, but I knew his timing always proved best.

Amy

I thought maybe if I just ignored it things would go back to normal. I tried to make sense of it, justify it almost. Was I hitting it too hard lately, partying every night? That was a given! Two grams of cocaine wasn't going as far for me as it used to. I told myself I was just getting run down and sick like before, that must be it!? I wasn't convinced.

I'd been sick every morning for weeks, and was late. I began to cry, the tears streaming down my face. I just kept thinking it wasn't possible, this wouldn't happen. If I just thought hard enough it would turn out not to be true! No, No, No, I screamed at myself, it's impossible; don't even think about it because it's not true!

Days went by, weeks went by. I was tired all the time. Throwing up every morning like clockwork, crying during every solitary moment. It couldn't be put off any longer. I needed to know for sure. It was one of the most difficult moments.

I waited the allotted three minute time I'd read on the box, then I waited four, then five, then six. I can't, I can't look at it. I knew what the result would be but didn't want to see the proof staring back at me. Finally, fearing that the results may not be accurate if I waited any longer, I walked into the bathroom with closed eyes. I opened them and saw double lines; my worst fears had come true.

The strength in my legs left me and I crashed to the floor. No, No, No, No . . . I kept repeating through my sobs. Oh please, God No!! I was crying so hard I couldn't catch my breath. The room was spinning; I had to get out of the bathroom. Crawling along the floor over the steps to the living room my tears wouldn't stop.

I was crying from a place deep down inside. A place I had kept locked up for so long was now open wide. My soul was raw with emotion. Loneliness, sorrow, pain, and despair, all came rushing out. It was too much for me to handle. Unable to stop the tears, I lay there on the floor curled up in little ball, holding my knees. I was crying for more than my situation. I was crying for my lost soul, my lost life. I was crying for the person that I had let myself become.

Hours later I awoke still on the floor. My face still wet, throat raw, and nose bleeding. I went to the washroom to clean myself up. Disgusted with the face that I saw staring back at me in the mirror, I began to cry again. "Keep it together," a voice inside my head said. "You can fix this, and no one will ever know. It'll be just like it never happened."

I shook the thought out of my head and mixed a strong drink, grabbed my stash and popped a hit of ecstasy. The thoughts in my head began to subside. I knew I didn't want to be left alone with them. Hands shaking and vision blurred, I called up a friend. Never being one to admit my problems, I told her I just wanted to party.

As usual within minutes my apartment was transformed into a club. My friends came out of the woodwork, drinks were poured, joints were rolled and the music cranked. While in my bedroom changing I closed my soul off, buried my emotions deep, and emerged as the Amy that everyone knew. I began to slip back into the mould that I allowed everyone else to shape for me. Inside I was slowly dying. My dark, dried up soul longed for fresh life-giving water.

SEVENTEEN

A RAY OF HOPE

Sharon

One week before Christmas, the family gathered to celebrate Amy's birthday. I was surprised when she arrived first. I hoped we could talk like we used to, but waited for her to make the first move. She surprised me by pouring out her frustrations and pain. Her boyfriend wanted to move in with her. She was lonely. Her life was a mess. Although she tried hard to change, she felt like a failure.

I saw a young woman choosing to make changes in her life, but still struggling to do it in her own strength. She was sure she could do it, but was proven wrong again and again. I hugged her and told her I loved her. I sensed she didn't want to hear more. I felt the resistance in her embrace. I hoped the message I repeated so many times would sink into her alcohol soaked brain.

As I prepared the meal, her favourite—lasagna with extra cheese, Caesar salad and garlic bread—I silently prayed through my tears, *Father, instill such a hunger in Amy's heart for you*

that she will leave her destructive life behind and trust you to
provide all she needs. Draw her into your comforting embrace.
Open her eyes to the Truth.

Amy
Journal Entry: December 23, 2001

Wrapped some Christmas presents today. This is the worst
Christmas ever. All I want to do is cry and throw up. Mom and
Dad are so excited that Julie's pregnant. Oh, and bonus, I just
found out today that Julie's friend Sara is pregnant too. I swear
every day I hear about someone else who's expecting. It makes
me want to scream. I can't stand it! The same news that makes
everyone else so happy brings me only agony and remorse. I'm
so sick of lying to everyone. Sometimes I can barely keep all the
lies straight in my head. All I want to do is cry and never stop.
What a sham my life really is.

Sharon

As the days went by and I didn't hear from Amy, I wondered
what was happening in her life. Two weeks later, the phone rang
as we are leaving for dinner with my sister and her husband.
The call surprised me. "Mom, I'm really sick. Been throwing up
every half hour since 2 a.m." Not one to ask for help, Amy gave
sketchy details. I knew something was dreadfully wrong.

We drove to her apartment immediately. One look at my
daughter and I decided to stay with her whether she asked or
not. Holding back the tears, I bathed her face and hands, and
helped her to the bathroom as she vomited over and over again.
Is this another reoccurrence of the flu? I wondered.

She seemed glad to see me, yet visibly uncomfortable that I was there. My heart lurched at the sight of her surroundings. The room was a mess—evidence of weed on the table, empty bottles and pizza boxes everywhere. I opened the refrigerator to put away the juice and fruit I'd brought, only to find more bottles of liquor, a stale piece of pizza topped with curled up pepperoni and a jug of cooking oil, but no food. The freezer was full of ice because the door wouldn't close properly. The kitchen counters were stacked with dirty dishes, and glasses swam in a sink full of cold, grungy water.

Anger and shock overpowered me. Disgust rose in my throat like a wave of nausea. I tried to convince myself that she really couldn't be living this way, there must be another answer. But I knew the truth already. It's always a slippery slope downward when self is on the throne, and God is pushed aside.

After making sure she was comfortable, I curled up on the couch. Outside, the raucous noises on the street pierced the darkness. I stayed awake most of the night expecting her friends to come barging through the door, ready to party at their familiar haunt. The flimsy lock on the door wouldn't keep out a gnat.

The stale, hot air assaulted my nose and the strange mixture of odors turned my stomach. As I stared at the dirty ceiling, I remembered that we had prayed over every room in this apartment, asking God to keep her safe. Now, I prayed that God's presence would permeate this place, making it difficult for her friends to feel comfortable here.

In the darkness I felt God draw near. *My daughter, you are still trying to blame Amy's friends for her decisions. Have you prayed earnestly for their souls? I love them as much as I love your daughter. My Son died for them.* I wept at his words.

I woke up hoping to find that everything we'd been through was a bad dream. The lingering sense of God's presence eased my aching heart as I realized it wasn't. I washed the dishes and scrubbed the kitchen, ignoring Amy's insistence that she could do it when she felt better. Keeping busy helped me to process the truth staring me in the face.

After a light meal of soup and a warm bath, Amy said she felt better. "Thanks for cleaning the place up," she said, not looking at me. An awkward silence hung between us like the charged moments between the flash of lightning and the crack of thunder. I wanted to ask her how a smart girl with everything going for her could end up addicted to drugs and alcohol. How could she stand living in a place like this? Could this be the reason she was sick? The questions remained unasked.

A range of emotions struggled within me. Anger, fear, sadness, and grief cried out for a voice. But they gave way as I looked at my daughter. Her eyes reflected the despair written on her face. I had an overwhelming desire to kneel down beside her and ask if she was ready to leave this destructive life.

"I've been thinking of moving home. Not right away. In a few months." The words came out tentatively as if she were afraid to say them. "I don't have any money for rent."

It caught me off guard. I was sure she would never want to move back home.

She's coming home! It's what I've been waiting for. I'll have her room ready in no time. She must be sick of this life. Is she ready to give her life to Christ?

A moment later, the positive thoughts turned negative as a barrage of questions rattled through my mind like gun fire. *Is she serious? How could it possibly work? Will she leave a four room apartment for one small bedroom? What about the music she listens to? What would Bill think? Is she planning on changing her lifestyle? What about the late hours? Would we go full circle and end up right back where we started? And why doesn't she have any money?*

"Mom?" Her voice broke into my thoughts. I realized I hadn't answered her question.

"When you left, we told you our door would always be open and you could come home any time." I knew what I said next could push her one way or the other. "We meant it. We'd love to have you come home." I thought I saw a flicker of relief as she raised her head to look at me. "Have you really thought about this? It will mean a lot of changes for both of us."

"I know."

When my husband arrived a few minutes later to drive me home, his face wore a pained look as he glanced around the room. I could tell it was all he could do to stay long enough to put plastic over a cracked window and fix the freezer door. I knew seeing his Amy in such a state broke Bill's heart. Leaving her there was unthinkable—but we must!

On the way home I shared with him what Amy told me. The news must have been like an injection of hope. The thought of his little girl coming home brought a smile to his face—the first I'd seen in a long time. I wondered if he had considered how much harder it would be to watch Amy's life up close again. We'd prayed for so long that God would accomplish his will in Amy's life. Could this be part of his plan?

EIGHTEEN

THE SECRET

Sharon

The dawning of the New Year brought more pain than joy. Usually our family spends New Year's Eve together. It's a night of fun and food, and seeing who can stay awake the longest. Often playing a board game, or watching a good movie kept us going until we paused at midnight to celebrate the beginning of the New Year with a toast of sparkling grape juice and another plateful of goodies.

This year, amid the laughter and retelling of the year's events, I tried to take part in the merriment but my heart ached. Amy wasn't with us. Our family was not complete. A deep sadness crept over me. I felt like I was running in slow motion, looking backward, trying to recapture something we had all lost.

In the morning, we stayed in our pajamas, enjoyed a breakfast of waffles and fruit, eggs and bacon, toast and coffee, and watched the Rose Bowl Parade. We've done this every year since the girls were little. As I stared at the screen, my mind drifted back over the years, recalling the times our girls would curl up on the couch beside me and watch the beautifully decorated parade floats pass by.

On days like this I wanted to retreat into the past, to happier times when they were young and life seemed simpler. We had family devotions together—or should I say, we tried to—but it was often sporadic. We always knew where the girls were, and we knew the kids they played with. As they left for school, I would hug them and pray for them before they ran to catch the bus.

Questions plagued me like a persistent insect buzzing in my ear. *Did we treat Amy differently because she was the youngest? Were we more lenient with her? Did the inconsistencies in our family devotions cause her to believe we didn't think they were important? Were we consistent in our Christian walk? Did we model Christlikeness before our girls?* I knew the answers to some of those questions and they made me cry.

Amy

For days I walked around heartbroken and confused, my mind constantly racing. I couldn't sleep; I couldn't think. I felt so lost I didn't know where to begin. I needed to talk to someone. I needed someone to put their arms around me, someone to help me, someone to love me. Little did I know that Jesus was standing outside the door of my soul, quietly knocking, longing to throw his loving arms around me.

I had become so lost I barely knew his voice. Instead of listening to his soft whisper, I bought into the lies. *He doesn't love you! Not anymore! Not after this.* I wanted to run to my mother and tell her, but my head was full of deception. *You can't! You can't tell anyone! What would people think of you? You've already put your family through so much, this would*

*break them. They don't deserve to be burdened with this. It's
your mess, you fix it.*

I tried to stop the constant battle that raged inside my head
but I couldn't. The lies just kept coming. *You would be a horrible
mother! You'd never be able to stay sober. How could you afford
a child? You can't keep it and marry him. You'll be stuck forever.
You'll be this woman you detest, this worthless, hopeless shell of
a person forever, trapped, living this life permanently.*

No. That wasn't going to happen to me. The lies started to make
more sense. *You only have one real option—have an abortion and
things can go back to normal. No one will ever find out.*

Day by day the lies chipped away at my spirit. Slowly my
strength of mind faded and I found myself considering an
abortion. I knew it was murder. I knew it was appalling. I knew
no one could ever know.

"Follow me, please."

I did as I was told and followed the nurse down the hallway
to a small curtained off bed.

"You can change into your gown here," she said. Pulling the
curtains shut, she marched down the hall.

I moved as if I were on autopilot, slowly undressing and
slipping into the gown. My mind was blank; my emotions
numb. I wouldn't allow myself to think or feel. Standing in the
small room I could hear the quiet sobs and whispered reassur-
ances of the couple next to me.

I wondered how many other babies . . . No! I won't think
of that. I can't think of that! I turned to the chair and started

olding my clothes. Without warning, the curtains were pulled open. "Follow me, please" the nurse said.

I followed obediently, noticing another woman in a gown as we passed. She glanced at me, and then her weepy red eyes stared at the floor as she followed her escort. I felt nothing when I saw her. I'd retreated into survival mode, doing what I felt I needed to do to survive this horrible experience.

We turned left and entered another room where five or more nurses busily checked gauges and adjusted instruments.

"Sit here." I did as I was told. The doctor made some comment about the weather. I said nothing. A nurse gently patted my hand and told me to relax. I stared blankly at the ceiling as a horrible noise filled the room.

My body burned with pain, but I didn't move. I couldn't take my eyes off the ceiling; I didn't want to take in all that was going on around me. I wanted it to be ten years earlier when I was a little girl fishing with my dad, happy, innocent and carefree, full of honesty and joy.

I couldn't face now. Not what I was doing; not what I'd become. Tears welled up in my eyes and poured down my cheeks. I couldn't hold them back. Before I knew it, I was sobbing uncontrollably.

"Hold her still," commanded the doctor. As the nurses held me, the crying slowly subsided and numbness closed over me.

As the nurse lead me down the hallway, my blank stare caught the eye of another woman in a gown. We said nothing, our eyes sad and hopeless. As I lay on the bed feeling nauseous, another nurse bustled in and injected something into my thigh, then gave me some pills. She left without saying a word.

I stared at the ceiling clutching my abdomen. It felt like my insides were on fire. I could hear the crying of women around me, but my tears had dried up. There would be no more tears for me, no more words spoken, no more emotions felt. I would lock this agony deep inside where it would never be thought of again.

NINETEEN

IN GOD'S HANDS

Sharon

Over the next few months Amy stopped by after work nearly every day. I couldn't read the expression on her face, but something had changed. Maybe she just needed the reassurance that the option of moving home was still open.

I looked forward to these visits when Amy gave snippets of information about what was going on in her life, doling out a piece here and a piece there like Hansel and Gretel leaving a trail of breadcrumbs. If they were clues marking her path, I wasn't sure where they were leading.

I found out she had been seeing a new guy, who eventually broke her heart and moved on. The downward spiral began again: heartbreak and disappointment. If that weren't enough, she lost one of her two jobs. I could see the enemy clapping his hands with glee. He was out to destroy our daughter. He laughed in our face while he danced his victory dance.

"I'm going to Daytona Beach with some of my friends on March Break." The announcement came two days later, clearly not requiring any input on my side. Alarm bells went off in my head loud enough to be heard across the room. I couldn't keep myself from asking, "Who's going?"

"Three girls and three guys," She saw the expression on my face. "Mom, I'm 22, not some 15-year-old kid."

Several days before the trip, Amy called to ask if I would come over and feed her cat. She casually mentioned that the other girls had dropped out and it was just her and the guys going. I felt physically sick thinking about what could happen. *Is her brain fried from the drugs? Is she able to think rationally at all? Has her heart been seared by sin so she can no longer hear God's voice?*

While I struggled to push my fears aside and pray, God patiently reminded me that I had agreed to leave her in his hands. I realized that my worrying exposed the truth. I was questioning God's ability to take care of my daughter. How could I do such a thing? The circumstances of life will either shrink or stretch your faith. I felt my faith shrinking and I knew I had to make a conscious choice to trust God at this moment and for all the moments to come.

For the whole week she was gone, I sat at my computer and stared at the screen, unable to write even though writing deadlines inched closer every day. All I could do was pray. I prayed when I felt God's presence, and when I didn't. I prayed while I drove to her apartment to feed her cat, Jeb. I prayed when I saw the evidence of her sinful lifestyle. I prayed through my tears.

I prayed throughout the day while I did the laundry and made meals, and while I sat in my favourite chair near the living room window, the one we call the 'waiting chair', and stared down the road, aching to see her returning home. Before

I closed my eyes in sleep, I finally put her back into God's hands once again.

The familiar words from a verse in Philippians came to mind. "Don't fret or worry. Instead of worrying, pray. Let petitions and praises shape your worries into prayers, letting God know your concerns."[21] How often had I quoted that verse to family and friends as an encouragement to trust God? Now, in my circumstances, they brought fresh insight for me as I read the words out loud, "Before you know it, a sense of God's wholeness, everything coming together for good, will come and settle you down. It's wonderful what happens when Christ displaces worry at the center of your life."[22]

A week later, I got a phone call. "Hi, Mom. I'm home. I loved the palm trees." No details, no chitchat. Who cared about palm trees? Yet simply hearing those words made me thankful she was home.

Maybe she'll tell me about her trip, maybe not. I'm learning not to pry. It's a process—and not an easy one. I resisted the urge to sit her down and grill her for information. I have to respect the fact that she is not a child—she's a young woman who is making her own decisions. I am hungry for the close and intimate relationship I once shared with my daughter. I long for our easy and open conversations, and our laughter. I miss hearing the excitement in her voice when she talked of someday owning a horse ranch where she could teach disabled children to ride. I miss crying over sad movies together. I miss my daughter.

Amy
Journal Entry: March Break 2002

Well this is easily the best spur of the moment decision the three of us have ever made! The boys and I are finally here at Daytona Beach! It only took 25 hours to get here, but we did drive straight through. We only stopped for coffee and gas. Hurray for cocaine, it keeps you going through the night!

So here I am watching a crappy movie in a smelly motel room. Jeff and Tom are passed out, but I'm too high to sleep. Got some coke from this guy I met on the beach. It's great, except we had to go to a strip club to get it. I don't remember what street we were on, but when we came out of the place there were like eight cop cars on the road, tons of people yelling and screaming. It was crazy! I felt like I was in an episode of COPS. I guess it's a pretty rough part of town. Anyway, somehow I managed to get through that okay. It's a good thing too since I had two g's of coke on me. So now I'm here writing this while everyone else is passed out. Good Times.

Sharon

We found out that one of Amy's friends was moving into her apartment when she asked her dad if he would come over and build the framework for a temporary wall. My curiosity prodded me to go with him and see what was going on. We arrived to find the same messy apartment filled with more suitcases and boxes.

Amy was quite proud of her idea—creating a second bedroom behind the couch by attaching a large roll of carpet underlay to a wooden framework. When I expressed my concern over such a flimsy wall serving as a bedroom for her roommate, Jennifer, she quickly corrected me. "I'm giving her my bedroom. I'll sleep here."

Anger mingled with fear as I thought about her dressing and undressing behind a makeshift wall with no door. *What are you thinking? What about when there are guys here? Why can't you share the bedroom? Have the drugs damaged your brain? Do you have any modesty left at all?* I wanted to demand answers to those questions, but what good would it do?

I tried to express my concerns in a reasonable manner, but I could tell by the look in her eyes that she was determined to do this. I left with a pounding headache, and I could tell from Bill's grim expression that he was fighting to control his emotions. What could we do to help our daughter see the destructive path her feet were stumbling on? She certainly wasn't asking for our advice. "God, I can't take much more," I groaned. *Love her unconditionally,* he whispered.

Journal Entry: June 13, 2002

It's easy to get so focused on difficult times that we miss the joys and blessings each day brings. All our worries were pushed aside when our son-in-law called to tell us that Julie was in the hospital in labor. We dropped everything and rushed to her room. There is nothing quite like the thrill of being grandparents for the first time.

The waiting was hard—nothing compared to what Julie experienced as she endured 18 hours of labor. I paced outside the birthing room like a nervous bridegroom, straining to hear the sound of our grandbaby's first cry. I tried to read a magazine, but it was impossible to keep my mind on the story. The hours crept by at a snail's pace.

I couldn't help but ask the nurses for a progress report each time they came from the birthing room. They kindly told me it wouldn't be long now, the same thing they'd been saying for hours. I found myself strolling close to the door that separated me from my daughter, hoping to hear something—anything.

Then, I heard it. A cry. The sound of new life. I am a grand-mother. I rolled the word around on my tongue, loving the taste of it.

After another hour of anxious waiting, a nurse told me I could go in. I will never forget seeing baby Adam for the first time as he was placed in my outstretched arms. I have a grandson and he is beautiful. My heart overflowed with thanksgiving for this precious gift from God.

Now all the details are of great importance. How did the delivery go? Were there any complications? How much does he weigh? How long is he? But as I looked into the face of my first born daughter, I realized that none of these questions needed answers right now. Julie had become a mother, and I a grand-mother, and all was well.

Holding this child in my arms, I am reminded again of God's faithfulness. I wanted to cradle him against my heart for hours, but I kissed his soft cheeks and reluctantly passed him to my husband who was waiting to hold his first grandson. He stroked his hair and said, "I can't wait until I can take you out fishing with me."

The grin on his face said it all as he smiled down at Adam. "Finally another boy in the family." My heart skipped a beat when I heard him singing the same song he used to sing to Julie when she was a baby. As I stored this memory in my heart, I prayed Adam would come to know Jesus as his Saviour early in life. What path, I wondered, has the Lord marked out for this beautiful baby boy?

TWENTY

FACING THE TRUTH

Sharon

"Hi Mom." Amy's voice sounded dull and listless on the phone.

"Hi, honey. What's wrong?"

In a monotone voice Amy filled me in on how her latest boyfriend had dumped her. "I feel like such a fool for believing in this guy." I thought I heard a sob. Unlike the other guys in her life, we had met this one a couple of times. He and Amy had come to church one Sunday morning because he said he wanted to know more about God. After the service, they insisted on taking us out for lunch.

"In September, I'm either going to Barrie to find a job, or I'm moving home. I haven't decided, but I need to get away from this apartment, from all the partying."

Anger bubbled up in me like hot lava. I wanted to shout into the phone, *it's those friends you've been hanging out with, the ones who introduced you to smoking, drugs and alcohol, the ones who crash at your apartment but never bother to clean up or help with the expenses. They got you hooked on this lifestyle. They . . .* The accusations repeated themselves like the steady dripping of a leaky faucet.

I dumped the blame on her friends to keep from facing the truth. The apartment was her responsibility not theirs. No one forced her to do anything. She made her own choices. We are all lead astray when we demand our own way, removing God from his rightful place and putting self on the throne of our life. Amy continued to walk away from the Truth, and she would have to live with the consequences. The thought made my stomach clench with dread.

As I hung up the phone, I gave in to the tears I'd been holding back. I wanted to hear the truth. I wanted answers. Was she using hard drugs? Where was she getting the money and what was she doing to get it? I refused to let my mind go further. I remembered watching an interview with a seventeen-year-old cocaine addict. She explained that the mental addiction to drugs was as powerful as the physical. Her insatiable appetite for the next fix to get her high blocked out all reason and became her reality. She would do anything to get that fix. Anything.

Would Amy end up in a drug rehab center? Would we lose her to a drug overdose? Would she die of alcohol poisoning alone in her apartment or in some dark alley? Black tentacles of fear entwined around my heart like an octopus trapping its prey. Why did I keep taking her out of God's hands? I certainly couldn't protect her.

I fell to my knees. "Lord, please speak to Amy. Put a wall of protection around her. Keep the enemy from his plan to destroy her. Please, Lord, please," I pleaded through my sobs, crying until my throat was sore and I had no tears left. I knew that ultimately she would make her own choices—even the choice to live or die.

On the following Saturday afternoon, Amy dropped by for a visit. It surprised me to hear her say she believed that her boyfriend leaving was an answer to prayer and that God was at work in her life. *Had our daughter been praying?*

"I've been praying that God would take him out of your life," I admitted. "I couldn't see how your relationship with him could be part of God's plan for you." I knew God's ways were far above mine and felt convicted that I had already written him off instead of praying for his salvation.

"My conscience has kept me from doing some things." She paused as if she didn't know how to continue. "I hear God's voice in my head. I can't even enjoy the things I want to do because I feel God is right there with me."

I open my mouth to speak and then close it again. This was a time to listen.

"I hear your voice too," she says. "I remember all those times you prayed for me at the door before I left for school, and all the things you and Dad have taught me."

"Honey, these are all answers to prayer. God is working in your life. I want to tell you a dream I had over a year ago. I asked God when I should share it with you, and I feel compelled to tell you today."

She listened intently while I described the dream exactly as it happened that night, reliving it again as I spoke the words.

"I awake with a start. My mouth is dry, my heart thumping in my chest. Fear is a palpable presence in the room. Dream images hang around me like thick draperies, threatening to smother me. I am fully awake now, my breathing shallow. I feel this experience is of great importance, something I should pay attention to. I believe God is telling me something about my daughter through this dream. I remember reading about Joseph. When he told his family about his dreams, the Bible says " . . . but his father kept the matter in mind."[23]

I close my eyes and recapture the images. Slowly the scene spreads itself over the screen of my mind like a movie in which I am the spectator. I am in a house, though not my own, looking through the kitchen window into the courtyard of another house nearby. I am surprised to see four young women walk through the door and seat themselves on a low bench along one wall. Their faces look as if they have been carved from white stone. They do not speak to each other. They do not look toward the sun, or glance at the flowers nearby.

They stare straight ahead as if waiting for something. Their eyes are dead, like those of a shark. I am startled to recognize my daughter among them. Just as I am about to call out to her, I hear a voice—chilling, authoritative, otherworldly—ordering them inside.

In a desperate attempt to get her attention, I shout to my daughter, "Amy, just walk toward me, come home. He can't keep you there. You don't have to obey him. You can leave. Just walk away."

I am held back by some invisible yet repulsive force. I cannot run to her, though everything in me aches to rescue her. She does not look up. The air is oppressive and thick with evil. I feel it creeping toward me. Upon hearing the voice, the girls rise as one and file back into the house—like timid sheep helplessly moving into the lair of a waiting lion."

Amy was silent for a few moments, tears trickled down her cheeks. "Remember back in the Youth group when God spoke to me and told me he had a special plan for my life? I've never forgotten that. It's been like an anchor in my life. No matter how far away from God I go, I still feel him pulling me home."

Disappointment welled up inside me. The dream had such an impact on me; I thought she would have a greater reaction. It portrayed a clear picture of her life. Was I expecting Amy to fall on her knees, weep uncontrollably, ready to repeat the sinner's prayer?

Then her words jolted me like I'd been t-boned in an accident. *I still feel him pulling me home.* Suddenly I felt elated. Those were the words I'd wanted to hear for so long. They were proof of God's great faithfulness, his unfailing love, his never-ending mercy. He was still calling her home. He would continue to do so. One day she would choose not to go back into the lion's lair.

We were both in tears as she told me her friends were asking questions about spiritual things. "I tell them what I know." she said. "They think I have all the answers because I was raised in a Christian home and they weren't. I tell them what I know is true, even though I'm not living it. I'm sure not a good example for them."

Before she left, I gave her my old Bible. It had many verses underlined and dated—promises that God made real to me over the years.

"I want to start reading the Bible again," she said, flipping through the pages. "I'm glad we can still talk. It helps me to piece together what's been happening in my life—to make some sense of it." With a quick hug she was gone as if she were afraid that if she stayed longer she would say too much.

TWENTY ONE

COMFORT ZONES

Amy
Journal Entry: September 19, 2002

I'm beginning to think that comfort zones are just another word for laziness, or perhaps it's just the scapegoat I use. Funny how everyone has a reason for their actions, for their lifestyle. Some people have a sad story to tell, one that they dwell on and can't get over. Some people have had more than their share of bad things happen to them, but with me, I suppose it's just laziness.

My life is a portrait that I painted with my bad decisions and I've become so accustomed to it that I haven't painted a new one. I desperately want one that I can show to people, that I can be proud of but I still don't paint.

Maybe it's like standing in front of a train, by your own free will, and ending up a quadriplegic in a wheelchair because of your decision. Now if you have determination and spirit, you could still learn how to paint with your mouth. Instead you choose to dwell on your stupid decision to stand in front of the oncoming train and refuse to think of anything except how you got yourself in this terrible mess in the first place. I guess that's me and my life in a way. Maybe that isn't a good analogy, but it's one that I understand.

Sharon

Sometimes making one decision can start a whole chain of events. Amy talked about moving home several times over the last few months. That's all I thought it was—just talk.

Then one day, in the middle of a conversation, she said, "Can I move home at the end of September? That's when my lease is up. I need to get my life straightened out." Her words rang with truth this time and I felt some of the weight I'd been carrying slip from my shoulders.

"Of course you can," I replied quickly. "What will you do with all your stuff? You'll be moving into one room and we don't have much storage space."

We both agreed that a yard sale would be the answer. Julie and Michelle offered to store some of her things. The following Friday, I went over to help her pack up her stuff. Working at two restaurants leaves her little time for much else, though I doubt she lets it interfere with her party life. *I'm glad you are getting out of this dump.* I stopped the thought before it came out of my mouth in words.

"What are you going to do with Jeb?" I asked as the small grey cat rubbed against my leg affectionately.

"Can't I bring her home with me?" I hear the pleading in her voice.

"Sorry. You know Sydney enjoys her 'only-cat-in-the-house' status. I think she'd end up in a psychiatric ward for aging cats if Jeb joined our family. Besides, two females usually don't get along well."

Her face told me that wasn't the answer she wanted to hear. "Okay, I'll try to find a home for her." She picked up Jeb and left the room. This was hard for her. It would be the beginning of many more hard things to come.

On moving day, we were surprised to see Jeff, her ex-boy-friend, waiting to help with the loading. The looks between them were filled with emotion. I thought he left her. I thought they were finished. How much of this life would come home with her, wrapped around her like a filthy security blanket, I wondered.

She lit a cigarette. I remembered the picture I took of her the day she moved into the apartment. Her face had a harder look now and her eyes no longer smiled. I thought I'd keep it as a 'before' photo, and put it beside the 'after' photo I would take when she committed her life to Christ.

While I carried out boxes, I tried to imagine what it would be like to have her home with us again. Besides finding space for all her stuff, we would all have a lot to work through. There would be adjustments on both sides. I knew that God had much more to teach me about unconditional love, patience, about trusting him completely and a thousand other things. When I think I'm doing well in any of the above, God throws in a little test to reveal my progress.

It was one thing to have our daughter living her life away from our home, but when she comes back we'll see and hear and know more than we'll want to. We are convinced this is what God wants us to do though it probably wouldn't make sense to anyone else.

I have to admit I felt twinges of regret about our empty nest days coming to an end. We had settled into comfortable routines, coming and going as we pleased with no thought of having to be home to make sure dinner was on the table. We ate when we wanted to, watched the movies we liked and I played my worship CD's as loud as I wanted to in a quiet house. I loved this new found freedom.

I enjoyed the tranquility of our home, situated in a rural setting bordered by woods, a farm field, and good neighbours on both sides. Birds added their melodious voices to the praise and worship music from the Christian radio station. What songs would be blaring from the bedroom at the end of the hall when Amy moved home?

Nothing could be more important than keeping the promise we made to our daughter 18 months ago when we told her our door would always be open for her return. It will mean change for all of us. How far would God push me out of my comfort zone and in what ways would he stretch me through this experience?

On Monday morning I awoke to a new odor in the house. It drifted into our bedroom like an unwelcome guest. Everything Amy brought home reeked of cigarette smoke. She was up early arranging her small space. I could see by her face this was difficult. The adjustment may take longer than she thought— longer than both of us thought.

For many years I've enjoyed having morning devotions in my favourite chair in the living room. God's Word has proven to be an antidote for fear and anxiety. Today the smell of smoke assaulted my nose and the chair was buried under boxes and clothes. As I stood with hands on hips, disgusted by the odor, I realized I had already blown God's first test on attitude. Though I hadn't said a word, and I could hardly admit it to myself, I resented this intrusion—this clash of two worlds. Without God's help, the adjustment period would be a disaster.

My offer to wash all her clothes was gratefully received. Within minutes they were piled in a small mountain outside her door. Thankfully they will dry on the clothesline. No man-made scent can compare to the smell of clothes dried outside in a brisk fall breeze. I wondered if the smoking and drugs had destroyed Amy's sense of smell, but I kept that question to myself.

Sydney, our over-weight Tabby, was happy to have Amy home. She followed her around, rubbing against her legs, purring for attention. A true animal-lover from childhood, Amy went from caring for small pets, to buying her own horse. She rescued Rytaio from a dull life. The retired race horse had been put out to pasture but Amy saw her potential. The scrawny horse with protruding ribs and infected ears blossomed under her patient and tender care.

We watched our daughter transform a skittish, abused animal into a confident hunter jumper that trusted in her commands. She poured her time and energy into caring for her horse, working hard to earn extra money to pay for her board and feed.

I thought of those years and wondered what happened to that girl? What started her down the road she ended up on? What would God use to get her attention and bring her back to himself?

Amy
Journal Entry: September 29, 2002

Moved my entire stuff home today. I have no idea where I'm gonna put everything, this room is so small. Oh well, at least this is free, no rent. I'm really gonna miss having my own space. It's sorta weird being here. I feel like it's a step in the right direction, but I'm still not sure if it's the direction I want to go. Well, at this point it's not really like I have much of an option. No more money means no more apartment.

TWENTY TWO

ONE STEP FORWARD TWO STEPS BACK

Sharon

The reality of our new life came into sharp focus as the days went by. It hit me like a jolt out of the blue when I carried three plastic bags full of empty liquor bottles to the recycling box at the end of our driveway. I had hoped we could have left them at the apartment to be picked up. What were the neighbours going to think when they drove by and saw this? Maybe they would laugh and say, "The Cavers have given up on God and gone on a binge. We always thought they were a little strange."

Disappointment and anxiety soon overshadowed the initial relief I'd felt when Amy came home. Now I had a front row seat to watch her self-destruct. I realized that the move had forced her to leave some stuff behind, but she came burdened down with a lot of invisible baggage.

It wasn't long before the phone calls began. I heard enough to know she would be spending a lot of time away from home. The ties to her girlfriends and to Jeff were more like steel anchor chains than strings.

The emotional roller coaster was up and running again. It peaked at the top of the run when Amy joined us for our family Thanksgiving with all her aunts, uncles, cousins and grandparents. It sped downward when she stayed away for several days, presumably with Jeff.

When she came home, I asked if she was seeing Jeff again. She told me she sometimes stayed at his house with his family. After years of blatant lies and deceit, how could I know where the truth ended and the lies began?

Journal Entry: Oct 18, 2002

"It's hard to know what to do, God. I ask for wisdom and patience as you continue to work in my daughter's life, yet the more I pray, the worse, it seems, things get. I'm beginning to understand that the part of Amy's life I see is like the tip of an iceberg. The greater part is still hidden from me—but not from you.

I'm praying that you will break the chains that bind her and place within her heart a hunger for you. It seems I've prayed this prayer a million times. I hope you are not tired of hearing it.

Your Word says that no one comes to you unless the Spirit draws him. Use circumstances in her life to speak to her. Cause things to happen that will get her attention. Use every experience to point her to the Truth. C.S. Lewis said, "God whispers to us in our pleasures, speaks in our conscience, but shouts in our pain . . . ."[24] Shout in her pain, Lord. Cause her to hear you. Woo her and win her back to the One who loves her so completely.

I'm choosing trust over fear again today, Lord. You have proven yourself faithful to me all through my life. Like the wise man, I am building my life on a solid, unshakeable foundation— the Rock, Jesus Christ. You are my anchor in the storms. My trust and my hope are in you.

I came home today to find Amy in tears, quite surprising for someone who likes to appear in control and does not easily give in to crying. I waited until she was ready to talk. When she started, the story spilled out from a place of deep hurt. She and Jeff have broken up—again. He's depressed and pushing her away. He's leaving town and wants her to come and live with him. She refused. A small victory.

Her heart was broken. How many times can a heart be broken, I wondered, before it is permanently damaged? It was hard to see her this way. All I could do was love her. She wasn't ready to hear any answers I have to give. I put my arms around her, holding her close like I did when she was a little girl, and silently prayed, *Father, please speak to her. Touch that place deep inside that is so wounded. Keep her from hardening her heart against you.*

My mother used to say, "I'm at my wits end." As children we never really knew what it meant, but there was no mistaking the tone in her voice. She'd had it. Enough! That's how I felt. I didn't want to hear one more time how Jeff had broken her heart. This was her life. She really didn't want my input.

When she left after getting a phone call, I knew Jeff had given her another sob story about how much he needed her. Why couldn't she see that he didn't really love her, that he was just using her? *What is it going to take to get her attention, God? I'm afraid of what the answer might be.*

Amy
Journal Entry: Oct 20, 2002

So here I sit, crying in the dark while Jeff is contently sleeping. What's the point of this? I drive over here thinking I want to be here, thinking I want to be with him. Then, I get here only to find out all he wants is sex. What's the point of this relationship? It's not a relationship at all. It's just a booty call. I end up sitting here feeling worthless and used. He gets what he wants, and what do I get? I get pain, pain, and more pain! I just wish I could be wanted for more than my body, loved for who I am. I can't take it any more. All I feel is disappointment and shame. This isn't a relationship; this is toxic.

TWENTY THREE

TRADITIONS

Sharon

Winter swept in and covered fall's colourful displays with a dazzling show of its own. A snow storm on the first of November blanketed the ground in sugary white crystals. Change was everywhere except in Amy's relationship with her boyfriend.

God spoke to my heart this morning while I was praying. "You are so concerned about Amy. How much time do you spend in prayer for her?"

The question surprised me. "Lord, you know I pray for her and all of our family every morning. I'm praying and believing that you will bring our daughter to repentance."

"Will you spend two hours every night praying for your daughter?" he whispered to my heart.

His Spirit had already been convicting me that worry had invaded my thinking and like an invasive weed in the garden that steals the soil's nutrients and blocks out the sunlight, it was robbing me of precious time spent in his presence. I'd allowed anxieties and fears to push hope aside far too often, leaving me vulnerable to the enemy's attacks.

How many times had my heavenly Father brought me back to this place? He put his finger on the things that would bring about growth and maturity in my life and asked that I submit them to his will. Like a stubborn child, I sometimes chose to ignore his prodding and resisted his pruning in my life, but today I chose obedience.

Journal Entry: November 20, 2002

Today would have been my mom's birthday. Memories flood my mind as I think of her. She loved her grandchildren and would have been thrilled with the news that Julie was pregnant. I'm glad she has been spared the pain of watching Amy's wayward life.

Tonight I am in my bedroom with the door closed. I know this time I spend with God will benefit me as much as my daughter. I read a verse from Proverbs that encouraged me. "He who fears the LORD has a secure fortress, and for his children it will be a refuge."[25]

Yes, Lord, that's what Amy needs—a refuge—a place of safety and rest. But how do I pray for her? I've asked you to speak to her, to bring about circumstances that will turn her heart toward you, to protect her from a lifestyle that will destroy her spiritually emotionally and physically. I've prayed so many times. Have my words become repetitious and meaningless?

I will pour out my heart once more, Lord. Then I will be still and wait in your presence.

As I waited, I felt led to fast for Amy. Fasting and prayer break the strongholds of the enemy in ways I don't fully understand. Lord, you know my heart. I will fast for my daughter until you give me a further word.

How I long to see her come back to God, accepting his love and forgiveness. What a day that will be! I can see it so clearly in my mind. All of heaven is rejoicing, and the angels are looking on in wonder as Amy comes home to her Father and is welcomed into his loving embrace.

I would remember Christmas of 2002 as bittersweet, full of laughter and tears. Beautiful lacey snowflakes swirled through the air, covering the trees in white robes and softly carpeting the ground, creating a haven of splendor and tranquility.

Amy asked if she could invite Jeff for Christmas dinner and we agreed. As much as we disagreed with their relationship, he was someone she obviously cared for. With three daughters we've seen a lot of guys come and go.

Again I felt the old urge to blame someone for Amy's behaviour. Today, Jeff was the target. *What new addictions had he introduced into her life?* He was a likeable guy, but I knew we were only seeing the tip of his iceberg as we were with Amy.

Parents want their children to grow up to be responsible citizens, well-mannered, well-liked, reflecting all the good training they have received. In reality, we want them to be good examples of how well they were parented. It's a reflection on us as mothers and fathers. In many ways we parents live our lives again through our kids.

We ask ourselves, "What will people think of me if you do that? Or go there? Or wear those clothes? Or hang out with those friends? We forget that after doing our best with God's help to instill his commandments and values into their lives, we must set them free and allow them to make their own decisions—even ones we don't agree with. It is painful to see your child walk away from everything you've taught them.

On Christmas day, I tried to push aside my concerns and keep my mind focused on preparing the meal. The turkey roasted to a rich golden brown. Its tantalizing aroma mingled with the smell of mincemeat pies, spiced apple cider and the spruce boughs decorating the table. The familiar refrains of Christmas carols drifting through the room were nearly drowned out with the sounds of laughter and animated conversation.

As I looked across the table I noticed something in Jeff's eyes. Was he recalling a long-forgotten memory, or was he hung-over? I saw Jeff as the enemy, but he was just as lost as our daughter, and just as loved by God.

Lord, you know I've prayed this before. Please take this guy out of Amy's life if their relationship leads her farther away from you. Let him hear and see something today that creates a hunger in his heart for you. Touch him with your love.

After the meal, we gathered in the family room and listened as Bill read the Christmas story, a tradition we've kept over many years. I never tire of hearing about the birth of Jesus and how Mary, his mother, "kept all these to herself, holding them dear, deep within herself."[26] As my husband prayed a blessing over our family, I could honestly say I felt at peace.

The opening of gifts has its own custom. Usually the youngest member of the family hands them out. After they've all been opened, we show each other what we received. This year, little Adam stole the show. At six months, he wasn't interested in his presents, but loved playing with the boxes. Why don't we give children boxes instead of spending all that money on toys, books and games? Cardboard boxes can spark a lot of creativity.

I looked around the room and counted my blessings. In a quiet moment my thoughts turned to Mom. She knew how to celebrate Christmas in style. Being with her family was the highlight of her day—any day. When she died at 67 of congestive heart failure, her passing left a huge hole in my life.

Mom, I've missed you so much over the years; missed coming to visit you, and missed our talks. I think it would break your heart to see what's happening to Amy. You loved your children and grandchildren so much, and always encouraged them to trust God.

If you can see what's going on down here, I know you'll be smiling as you watch little Adam, your first great-grandchild, and all our family celebrating Christmas together. I'm looking forward to the day when we'll all celebrate together in heaven with Jesus.

I miss you.

TWENTY FOUR

WARFARE

Sharon

My first project of the New Year was to refinish an antique sewing cabinet given to us by Bill's mother. My attraction to old things, things with a history and character, has added some interesting and unusual pieces to our home. I thought of the woman who would have used the sewing machine the cabinet held, and wondered what kind of life she lived so many years ago.

Did she worry over her children? Did she sew clothes for her daughter, working late into the night to finish a dress for a special occasion, only to have her burst into tears because it wasn't like the ones the other girls were wearing?

Being a parent has never been easy. Today, as I sanded the cabinet and watched its beautiful wood grain appear, I thought of the Carpenter of Galilee. He worked with wood in his father's shop, planing the rough edges, shaping the piece with a chisel, and sanding the surface until it was smooth and perfect.

He works much the same in our lives if we allow him access to our hearts and submit to his hand. He uses the troubles and trials that come our way like sandpaper, removing the old layers of our self-life to allow his likeness to show through.

I've been feeling the grittiness of his sandpaper in my life a lot lately. Old patterns of thinking, familiar fears, my self-centeredness and the lies I've believed as truth are being gradually stripped away as Jesus works to reveal the beauty of his character in the cabinet that is my life.

Amy had only been home three months and already I felt like a race horse champing at the bit, wanting to share with her the Scriptures God had been showing me. Again he reminded me to love her unconditionally and leave the rest to him, bringing this verse to mind, "Wait for the LORD; be strong and take heart and wait for the LORD."[27]

Waiting has never been my strong point. Impatient and impulsive by nature, I'd rather do something than wait for something to happen, even if I have to make it happen. I think that's why God impressed me to pray and love, not march in and control Amy's decisions. More than anything, I didn't want to get in the way of what God was doing in her life. I wanted to compliment what he was doing. What were my mere words compared to the moving of his Holy Spirit?

Although we caught glimpses of change in our daughter, we still saw far more of the 'I'll-take-control-of-my-life' attitude in Amy. I thought when she came home she would cut the ties to her friends and come back to church, but that didn't happen. It seems she can't say no to them whenever they call. My hopes were dashed every time she left the house. For years I'd been living the first part of the verse, "Hope deferred makes the heart sick, . . . " I longed for the last part to happen—"but when dreams come true, there is life and joy."[28]

"Have you got any good books I can read?" Amy asked one day. This she asks of a writer? It came as a surprise, but I quickly handed her Randy Alcorn's, "Safely Home," a book I've read several times. I jumped right in and gave her the synopsis, telling her how much I enjoyed it, and how she would find this and that part of the story interesting.

Failed again. If that was another test, Lord, I blew it. I wanted to "do" instead of letting you speak to her heart in your own way. I could hear God's still, small voice reminding me. *Sharon, I love Amy far more than you ever could. You can trust her to me.*

Amy presented me with a beautiful bouquet of pink roses on my birthday. With the flowers came a card that expressed her love, and an invitation to have lunch with her. The gesture touched my heart. I saw a longing in her eyes and felt a difference in her hug. I wondered what was going on inside.

The following Sunday, she went to church with us. My hopes soared. I noticed that she cried throughout the service, something she hates doing in public. Several people came over to give her a hug. She told me later that she felt centered out, but I believe the hugs spoke to her.

After lunch, she wandered into the family room and opened up a little. "I was crying because of Jeff. I've been thinking about how bad my life is and how hard it would be to change." We talked for awhile. I assured her that she couldn't change on her own, but God would help her if she asked him to. She said "I know" in a way that suggested the knowing wouldn't be followed by doing. I believed God was speaking to her as clearly as he did when she heard the church bells on the Saturday night that she described as 'the worst night of my life'. I prayed she would listen this time.

The next day I found her reading the book of Revelation. I knew these changes in her were a direct result of prayer. So many people had been praying for our family. Some knew more of the story than others. Every time someone told me God brought Amy to mind, and they prayed for her, I felt encouraged. That's the family of God in action—bearing one another's burdens.

Our pastors, Frank and Maureen Patrick, have supported us in prayer from the beginning of our painful ordeal. Their friendship and genuine compassion provided a refuge where we could safely share the details of Amy's sordid life, vent our anger at the enemy and express our grief. We love them deeply and hold them in high esteem. Their ministry at Calvary Church is marked with faith, vision, passion, integrity and wisdom. We are blessed by their devoted leadership.

Bill spent endless nights wrestling in prayer for his youngest daughter. Since Amy now occupied the guest room, he prayed in the living room. Early in the morning, I would hear him getting ready for work. When I got up later, I found his Bible lying open on the couch and a box of tissues close by. I was sure he hadn't slept. When he came home from work, we talked again about our concerns for Amy and the attacks of the enemy on our own lives.

He pulled me into his warm embrace. "We're in a battle," he told me. "The enemy is fighting for her soul. If I have to work without sleep, I will." For both of us, having Amy living at home proved to be the best of times and the worst of times; the best because we loved having her close, and the worst because every decision she made to continue walking away from God hurt us deeply.

I love the story of the prodigal son. When his son left home, his father let him go. He didn't chase after his boy and drag him home. He loved, he watched and he waited.

He waited until his son found himself in a pigpen and came to his senses. When he came home, his father ran to meet him, welcomed him back with open arms and threw a party to celebrate his return.

Amy is not openly defiant or disrespectful, but we know she is living two different lives. I am convinced we live in two different realities—the truth and what we as parents think is the truth. My heart is raw from the lies. This morning, Amy picked up my old Bible that I'd given her when she moved to the apartment. She told me she found the note I had slipped between the pages. When she opened the Bible at random and began to read the underlined passages, she said they were exactly what she needed to hear. *Thank you, Lord. Hearing that she's reading your Word encourages me.*

Tonight, the pull of the party life with her friends sent her out the door. Would she remember the verses she read? I'd had a glimpse of the other life she was living, and wondered how much longer before she found herself in the pigpen eating slop?

The summer months passed in what had now become a predictable pattern. Her on-again-off-again relationship with Jeff left her smiling one week and crying the next. When she was home, she went to church with us, seemingly interested. Most week-ends, I suspected, were spent partying with her friends. *How much longer, Lord, before she ends up in the pigpen gagging on the husks?*

In the evenings, I tried to find ways to spend time with Amy. She loved jigsaw puzzles. Concentrating on something helped her mind to rest. My mission: to find the most difficult puzzles—snow scenes, fields of daisies, seascapes—anything that made it a challenge for both of us. We had some of our best talks while working on a puzzle.

Once in awhile we found that a piece was missing. Even with all the other pieces in place, the puzzle wasn't complete. Like our family, each member is unique and fits together with the others to make a beautiful picture. If one is missing, the picture will never be complete. Did Amy see that message in the puzzle? Even though she was with us physically, her heart had taken up residence somewhere else. Our family felt fragmented. A piece was missing.

I struggled with the thought that when she talked about God working in her life she did so because she was good at telling us what she thought we wanted to hear. At times, when it seemed that the enemy of her soul was winning the battle, I would come across a verse like this: "I have strayed like a lost sheep. Seek your servant, for I have not forgotten your commands."[29]

Would Amy pray this prayer one day soon? I know The Good Shepherd will never stop seeking his lost sheep.

Amy
Journal Entry: June 23, 2003

This will be the start to a whole new chapter of my life. Time to figure out what I want out of it, not what somebody else needs me to be. Jeff and I are over, finished! Chances are pretty good that he will try to call sometime within the next couple of weeks, but I've decided that this time I will end it for good. I'm not going to see him, call him, or talk to him on the phone. It's over. I won't be his friend either because every time this happens he ropes me back into the relationship, until he doesn't want a girlfriend—then we break up. I can never change the fact that I love him, but hopefully in time it will fade. So this is the start of one month without Jeff. It's going to be tough, but each day it will slowly get easier.

So my life is actually kind of exciting, knowing that I can do whatever I want now. There are no more distractions. I can explore my faith and become closer to God, which ultimately is Life. I will pray every day for strength and wisdom, and with his help, change the rut that my life has become for a wonderful adventure. I guess you could say I have lost love to gain Love!

TWENTY FIVE

WATCHING GOD AT WORK

Sharon

Life can change in the blink of an eye. On an ordinary day in August, during a heat wave that left the air motionless and stifling hot, life changed in a way few people would forget. At approximately 4:15 pm, 50 million people across Ontario and parts of the U.S. found themselves without hydro, making it the largest power failure in North American history.

Battery operated radios brought us sketchy details of the widespread power outage. Transportation ground to a halt as traffic lights blinked out in the cities. Subways and streetcars stopped. People found themselves trapped in elevators. Gas stations and grocery stores closed, leaving those in search of food, water and fuel with empty hands and empty tanks. No one knew how long the blackout would last.

With the light fading, we cooked our meal on the barbeque, and hoped the food in our refrigerator wouldn't spoil. We read by candlelight, like our ancestors, enjoying the break from electronic entertainment. At 12:30 am, we awoke with a start as the lights blinked on. The clocks beside our bed flashed, and music blared from the kitchen radio.

It will be an ordinary day when Christ returns for his church. That day will catch many unprepared, and life as we know it will stop. The world will be thrown into complete chaos as millions of people simply disappear. The thought gripped my heart. *How many of your neighbours will be left? Have you been a faithful witness of God's love and mercy? Are they prepared for the day when this mere power failure will be a miniscule glitch in comparison to Christ's return?*

As we gathered in the sanctuary on Sunday morning, those questions still weighed heavily on my heart. I looked around at the familiar faces and wondered how many had unsaved loved ones they were praying for. Why do we isolate ourselves in our times of greatest need? Why is it so hard to reach out and share our burdens with each other?

Thinking of Amy brought a fresh flood of tears, my heart ached with longing. *Will she come back to God? Will the rapture take place while she is still living in rebellion? What if she is left behind?* I recognized the enemy's attempt to plant seeds of doubt. "She *will* come back to God." I ground out the words through clenched teeth, furious at his deceiving tactics.

Fear threw its oppressive cloak over my shoulders. I have worn this garment for many years, but today I noticed it was easier to push it aside and ask God to cover me with his Truth. *Lord, let me not be so absorbed in Amy's waywardness that I forget to pray for others who are yet unsaved. Teach me how to show your love to them.*

While pulling weeds in my garden the next day, I couldn't help but think of The Master Gardener. He has been at work in the soil of my heart again, digging out the deep, stubborn roots of fear. The roots of invasive plants must be completely destroyed. If one small part is left, new shoots will spring up and overrun the garden. When the soil is free from weeds and smoothed by the Gardener's hand, he plants seeds of faith in the prepared ground.

Like a dazzling sunrise bursting over the horizon and dispelling the darkness, God gently reminded me of the dream he gave me over two years ago. As it replayed in my mind, I knew Amy would be saved. It may or may not be in my lifetime, but she would come back to God. Our lost child would reach for her Father's hand, the nail-scarred hand he has been holding out to her all this time. It may be in the worst circumstances of her life, but it would happen.

Early in September, our pastor announced that the Alpha Course would be starting in a few weeks. Bill and I taught one of the small groups during the last series, and had the opportunity to meet new people. Many who had little or no church background commented that they enjoyed getting to know each other during our meal times together.

As I listened to the sermon, God spoke to me in a voice that couldn't have been more real if it had been audible. *Invite Amy and her friends to Alpha.*

Amy and her friends? I questioned. *Would they come?* These were the girls I'd been praying for since their school days, the ones Amy hung out with. The next morning, I tried to pick the perfect moment to ask the question.

"Amy, would you like to go to Alpha with me? It's a ten-week video course on the basics of the Christian faith and it's presented by Nicky Gumbel, an Anglican priest," I blurted out all in one breath.

"Sure," she replied. I was elated, though her instant response surprised me.

"Your friends, too. Will you invite them?" She agreed so quickly I thought she hadn't heard the question.

I've been working in her life just as I'm working in yours. I'm preparing the soil of her heart to hear my words. Of course. That explained the instant response. God was way ahead of me.

I knew we were in for the fight of our life. Not with each other, but with the enemy. He would throw all kinds of obstacles in her way to make it impossible. I prayed all that day, asking God to create a hunger in her soul that only he could satisfy, and that the life she was living would become like the taste of ashes in her mouth.

On the night of the first meeting, Amy had to work later than usual. When she arrived home, instead of making excuses why she couldn't go, she hurried to get ready. During the meal before the video session, she said little and didn't make eye contact with those around her. I thought she might be regretting her decision.

She watched the video intently. I noticed the expression on her face change when Nicky talked about Jesus dying for our sins because of his great love for us. There were tears in her eyes.

Over the weeks that followed, she still went out on week-ends, but never missed an Alpha session. She told me she had invited her friends, but only one seemed interested in coming. I saw her reading her Bible more and we had good discussions on what the verses meant. I prayed that the hard shell she had built around her soul was beginning to crack.

One evening as we drove home from Alpha, she was especially quiet. I didn't expect her to talk. I could tell she was deep in thought.

"I'm having trouble forgiving myself for some of the stuff I've done," she said, her voice quavering. She grew quiet again. "I'm not having as much fun as I used to when I go out." Another long silence. "But I don't want to drop my friends. They'll think I'm a snob."

Journal Entry: October 16, 2003

Amy and I had a long talk after Alpha tonight. The session was on the importance of prayer. She tells me she notices her life is changing. She hears God's still, small voice a lot and feels guilty when she doesn't obey him. She thanked me for inviting her to Alpha and said it was just what she needed. The timing couldn't have been better. I am left to fill in the empty spaces as she gives me brief glimpses of what's going on in her heart and soul. I am so thankful I obeyed God's leading.

Her excitement is thrilling to see as she tells me she wants to go on a short-term mission's trip next year. *Shouldn't you be living a Christian life if you're going on a trip like that?* I stopped the words before they came out of my mouth. God is at work in her life, I reminded myself. Do your part: love her and pray. Leave the rest to him. It's so easy to say and do things that will interfere with God's purposes.

Her whole countenance has changed. She's reading Romans and often seeks me out to share the truths she's finding there. She tells me God is speaking to her through his Word.

She's coming to church more regularly, making it a priority, changing her hours at work so she can be there. It's wonderful to see evidence of God at work in our daughter's life.

A niggling thought steals in and snatches some of my joy. *What might the enemy do to keep her under his control?* I know he won't give her up without a fight. We must continue to persevere in prayer, interceding for our daughter. *Lord, put a hedge of protection around her.*

Amy
Journal Entry: October 18, 2003

Well, last night I did something I've never done before. I flushed the last of my X down the toilet! Even when I write that down I can barely believe it. God, you must be doing something in my head. The crazy thing is when I went into the bathroom to take them, I pulled them out of my pocket and I realized I didn't want them. I looked at them and thought to myself, *No . . . no more . . . no!* And I flushed them away. Now, with it being Saturday morning, I wish I could get them back. Oh, well, I guess it's a step in the right direction. You're gonna have to help me through this God, it's harder than I thought . . . way harder!

TWENTY SIX

DEFINING MOMENT

Sharon

As long as I live, I will never forget November 2, 2003. It will be etched forever in my memory as a tribute to God's redeeming love and great faithfulness.

Amy got up early enough to feed the animals at the pet hospital where she worked and still have time to get ready for church. She was determined to go with us every Sunday. We didn't know that this Sunday would be such a memorable day.

Pastor Frank preached a challenging message on our statement of faith—focusing on the Lordship of Jesus Christ in our lives. After his message, he said we were going to do something different that Sunday. Communion would be served to the congregation while those dealing with Lordship issues in their lives were invited to come to the alter where he and his wife, Maureen, would pray for them and serve them communion.

When the bread and juice were passed to our row, Amy didn't partake. I glanced in her direction. A mask of tension covered

159

her face. I bowed my head, praying that God would assure her once again of his love and give her the courage to go forward.

I felt her shift in the seat beside me. *God, let this be her moment,* I prayed. The war raging inside as Satan fought to keep control must have been powerful. I felt her move again. When I looked up, she was on her feet.

She walked slowly to the front as if her feet were made of lead. My heart leapt with joy. Tears streamed down my cheeks. All the memories of sleepless nights, all the fears that she might die of a drug overdose or alcohol poisoning, all the anguish of not knowing where she was or what was happening to her were swept away in that glorious moment.

When I saw her standing with her hands raised, I realized I was witnessing the fulfillment of the promise God gave me in the dream I'd had on April 27, 2001. I wanted to shout for joy. This young woman who didn't like drawing attention to herself stood in front of hundreds of people completely lost in the presence of God. Several ladies came to pray with her. Thankfully ours is a welcoming church—offering hospitality, healing and hope to everyone—even to a prodigal.

As she stood at the alter I pictured the nail-scarred hands of Jesus removing her filthy, ragged clothes and placing a clean white garment around her shoulders. She had been washed in the blood of the Lamb and made a new creation in Christ.

The Good Shepherd had found another lost sheep and brought her into the safety of his fold. Our prodigal daughter came home to Abba Father and he welcomed her with open arms. All of heaven was celebrating and rejoicing with us.

We didn't know that the greatest battle was still ahead.

Amy

It started the same as most Sunday mornings. I got up early and went to work, breaking the speed limit to get there so I would have enough time to get ready for church later. When I got there Buddy's kennel was a mess. The sickly old Golden Retriever had sprayed his whole kennel with diarrhea. I considered calling home to let Mom and Dad know I wouldn't be making it to church. But as I put Buddy in the bath tub a vague sense of today's significance came over me. I began to work faster. Washing, scrubbing, and cleaning. Checking I.V. lines and giving medications. Before long everyone was clean, comfy, and warm. I gave Buddy one last scratch behind the ears as he happily munched away at his breakfast.

"Almost ready? It's time to go" I could hear Mom asking from the kitchen.

I rushed to put on something semi-nice, something that wasn't too tight or revealing. I settled for an old dress and threw my hair into a quick pony tail.

"Ya, I'll be right there" I said grabbing my Bible and purse.

As we sat in our customary spot in the pew, it struck me that people really are creatures of habit. *Maybe that's why I'm having such difficulty changing things in my life?* I thought to myself. It was so hard lately, I was so sick of everything. I felt like I kept hearing God say, "Cut the strings and be free, free of everything that chains you." But I can't seem to do it. As I sat thinking to myself, I heard Pastor Frank say, " . . . until Jesus is in his proper place as LORD of our lives we will not succeed. We cannot serve two masters."

It became so clear to me. *Of course, of course, that's why I'm failing. I've been trying to live both lives, trying to please both groups. Too afraid that if I let the old me go completely, nothing will be left. Too afraid to give my all to him. God forgive me, I have wanted so many things more than I have wanted you.*

I knew in that moment that my whole life I had been telling God that he wasn't enough. He wasn't exciting enough for me. He wasn't real enough for me. The picture of Jesus on the cross, his body bloody and mangled, formed in my mind. *I put him there; what I've done has put him there. He took what I deserved.*

Before the pastor even said the words I knew I would be at the altar standing in front of everyone. He gave the invitation for those who needed Jesus to save them to come forward for communion. I went. My feet felt heavy as I moved down the aisle, my vision was blurred through tears.

"Forgive me, Jesus, forgive me," I whispered through my sobs. As I stood at the front I began to feel a warm embrace around me. Tears poured down my face as my nose ran. With no thought for how I looked or who was watching I raised my hands high, and thanked the One who never left my side.

Sharon

The last few Alpha sessions have been especially meaningful to Amy, especially the one on "Resisting Evil". She said it answered a lot of her questions. The following week, she found the courage to give her testimony in the small group. It was a big step. I had tears in my eyes as I heard her share some things about her life and speak of her determination to serve God wholeheartedly.

A few days later while we were having lunch, she asked me if I'd ever heard God's voice.

"I've never heard an audible voice, but his voice *is* real," I said, watching her face. "It's like his words resonate in your soul. And the more time you spend with him, the more you'll know his voice when you hear it. It's like sheep knowing their shepherd's voice. They recognize it and can distinguish it from all others. It is familiar to them."

"I think I heard his voice once," she said. "I was walking in my favourite spot and I heard him say, *Amy, cut the strings and be free.*" She paused for a moment. "I know what it means."

Journal Entry: November 4, 2003

Bill is away on a hunting trip so I don't have anyone to share my concerns with. After a day of glorious victory on Sunday, Amy went out with her friends last night. I can't believe it. Is she walking back into her old life? Doesn't she realize she has to rely on God's power in her life to break away from the friends she's been with for so long?

What kind of a hold do they have on her?

I spent the whole day in my bedroom, crying, praying, and asking God for answers. I let doubt consume me. I confronted her when she got home from work, asking why she stayed out so late. I knew my attitude was wrong.

It wasn't what I expected at all. The girls all went horseback riding and then spent hours talking about the changes they've seen in her life. She answered their questions using some of the illustrations from the Alpha course.

I jumped to wrong conclusions again, assuming the role of judge and jury, sentencing her before I heard her testimony. I think her life of lies has made me wary. Lord, forgive me for choosing doubt over trust—in you and in her.

We spent the evening together, enjoying the close and comfortable relationship we used to have as mother and daughter. Tonight it's so much sweeter. I showed her my prayer journal, and together we saw how God had answered our prayers concerning her, in very specific ways. How thankful I am for our family and friends who loved us lavishly and undergirded us with prayer.

Amy committed her life to Christ Jesus, accepting him as Saviour and Lord. Surrendering her will was the part she struggled with. Now, she will learn day by day how to walk in God's will and listen to his voice. She has started on a life-long journey with the One who loves her perfectly.

Amy
Journal Entry: November 28, 2003

So I write down all these pearls of wisdom that I gather from the Bible, but then I shut the book and put down the pen . . . and what I've written seems to vanish. My life goes its own route and I start doing all the same things I know I shouldn't. Destructive, horrible, selfish things!! I can't seem to connect the pearls I've found in the Bible to my everyday life. I'm almost becoming a split personality.

Sometimes I feel like I'm in a wearing down process, the good pieces of my heart are slowly withering. Probably for two main reasons: I don't listen to them and I don't nourish them. Nothing can survive in a black room with no door. Somewhere along the way I've lost the key.

I suppose if I'm honest with myself I know what I need to do to get it back, but can I change my life? Do I really need to cut all the strings, Lord? What will be left of me if I do? I think that's what scares me—letting go of everything! Who will I be if I'm not the tough, unbreakable girl who can do anything?

I read my Bible, I go to church, I write down insights and devotionals. Can't that be enough? The other part of me, the bigger part of me it seems, wishes I could just be content with my life the way it is.

To hell with it, this is too hard. I don't want to change! But I can't shake the fact that deep in my heart I know; if I continue on this road, I'll die. I feel this anxiousness and fear—this almost constant panic. I know I can't keep saying "yeah, I'll change my life, just not right now." I can't just keep sitting on the fence. Half of me a Christian; half of me a hopeless addict.

TWENTY SEVEN

CELEBRATING GOD'S FAITHFULNESS

Sharon

With Christmas only a few weeks away, the whole family got together for our traditional tree decorating party. We enjoyed watching Adam's fascination with the lights on the tree. He's 17-months-old, and a very busy boy. The breakable decorations were hung on the higher branches, leaving the others for his chubby little fingers to rearrange.

I get excited about Christmas, but nothing compares to the joy of seeing Amy accept Jesus Christ as her Lord and Saviour. The transformation we are noticing in her life is beautiful to see. I've been living in the afterglow of that November Sunday.

When she went out with her friends last night, I shook my head in disbelief. She told me that God had asked her about her motive for praying for their salvation. She had to admit she didn't want to lose their friendship. *Were these friendships so important that she would risk being entrapped in her old life again? And was it really friendship or were they testing her to see if her words and actions lined up?*

This morning she stayed home from work. When I asked why, she hung her head and told me she drank too much and had been throwing up through the night. I felt like I'd been hit by a train. The impact of her words pierced my heart like a knife. She's still drinking. Still going to bars. Still hanging out with the "wrong crowd". Why? Why? Why?

God's gentle voice interrupted my tirade. *Don't judge her. I am working in her life. Remind her of my forgiveness and my love. Have you forgotten how many times you've needed my love and forgiveness? Be my arms and hold her. Be my lips and share my truth with her.* I bowed my head, humbled and ashamed of my attitude, and asked him to forgive me—again.

Sitting on her bed, I shared some examples from my own life of times when failure had led to despair and I had believed the enemy's lies.

"You made a bad decision. Ask for forgiveness and go on," I tell her. "It's in the past now. Don't beat yourself up and don't feel condemned. God will convict you but he never condemns you. Jesus took all your condemnation on himself when they nailed him to the cross. He became your substitute."

She listened without comment. "Most important of all, don't let the enemy convince you it's easier to go back to your old life. Simply ask God to forgive you, then accept his forgiveness. Don't turn away from the One who loves you so much."

I reached for my Bible and read to her from a small piece of paper I keep tucked between its pages.

"Watch your thoughts; they become words.

Watch your words; they become actions.

Watch your actions; they become habits.

Watch your habits; they become character.

Watch your character; it becomes your destiny."[30]

Lord, please remind her of your unfailing love in tangible ways. Help me to do the same.

That night, Jeff called twice. "He wants me to come over and talk about our relationship," she said, hurrying to get ready. She told me he had left a gift for her at work—a beautiful watch. To me it was an obvious ploy. I assumed her recent failure had left her feeling vulnerable and I was all ready to tell her what to do. The gentle prodding of the Holy Spirit reminded me the decision had to be hers. So I said nothing, and prayed instead. *Father, help me to discern your wisdom and direction.*

It was almost the end of another year and I paused to reflect. What an amazing year. As I considered the faithfulness and blessings of God, the words from an old hymn came to mind. "All I have needed Thy hand hath provided." I discovered that Thomas Obadiah Chisholm wrote *Great Is Thy Faithfulness* as a result of his morning by morning realization of God's personal faithfulness. He wrote, " . . . I must not fail to record the unfailing faithfulness of a covenant-keeping God, for which I am filled with astonishing gratefulness."[31] That's how I felt. I cannot comprehend the faithfulness of God to one so undeserving as me.

When I thought back over the year, the picture that came to mind was a wall—a wall built by laying brick upon brick. Each of those bricks represented a specific time when I saw the faithfulness of God. The cement that holds them together is the character of God. God is always faithful. He never changes. Joshua reminded the Israelites of that when he called a leader from each tribe to pick up a stone and place it in the dry Jordan riverbed as a memorial of God's faithfulness to them. When the water level was low during times of drought, they could see the pile of stones. It seems we've been living in a drought for the last few years and I'm seeing clearly those stones of remembrance in my life. They inspire hope.

My journal is a testimony of answered prayer. The very best has been Amy's salvation. When I see her worshipping with her hands raised and tears in her eyes, I believe she is sincere. I think of the woman who washed Jesus' feet with her tears. Jesus said those who are forgiven much, love much. Truly Amy has been forgiven much. Her brokenness and contrite spirit are evidence of her love.

She tells us she has left the drugs and cigarettes behind but still goes out with her friends because she doesn't want to abandon them. As a Christian, she wants them to understand the reason for the changes in her life.

I believe she is still drinking. Her addiction to alcohol holds her in its unyielding grip, squeezing tighter and tighter like the coils of a constrictor, threatening to crush her, determined to smother the new life she's found in Christ. The same Serpent that succeeded in deceiving Eve is preying upon our daughter.

"If she feels unloved, Father, would you remind her again how much you love her and how very precious she is to you? Please, break this bondage. Teach her to ask you for help and to trust you completely. Thwart any plan of the enemy to ensnare her again and speak to her daily of the dreams and plans you have for her life." I prayed the words with renewed confidence in the presence of my Abba Father.

I have to admit I wondered what would happen on New Year's Eve. Would she go out to celebrate? Before the rest of the family arrived, Amy told me she didn't want to miss out on the fun. Throughout the evening her friends called but and she held firm in her decision to stay home and miss the biggest party night of the year.

At midnight we all raised our glasses of sparkling grape juice and toasted the New Year. I looked around the room and thanked God again for my family and for the happiness we found in being together.

My cup of blessing overflows. Bill and I have enjoyed thirty two years of marriage. Our two oldest daughters are married. It is thrilling to see God working in their lives, always drawing them into a deeper relationship with him.

Our grandson, Adam, is a constant source of delight. Tonight, I sang 'Jesus Loves Me' to him and rocked him to sleep. As his eyes closed and his long lashes brushed his pink cheeks, I whispered a prayer for God's blessing on his life.

No resolutions for 2004. I'm learning to live one day at a time. The past year has been difficult both emotionally and physically. I have prayed and cried over our lost daughter, often fearing for her life. My emotions have soared with hope and plunged into despair.

The physical pain from the compressed and degenerating vertebrae in my back is nothing compared to the anguish I feel when I realized Amy is still addicted to alcohol. Over the year, we have seen countless answers to prayer and God's intervention many times in Amy's life. The happiness I felt at her birth is surpassed by the joy I experienced when she was born into the family of God two months ago.

The dark clouds that formed an impenetrable covering over our lives for so long have disappeared and the sun shines down in dazzling brilliance. God holds the future in his hands. I will trust and not be afraid.

TWENTY EIGHT

I'VE CUT THE STRINGS

Sharon

On a bitterly cold January night Amy and I went to see a production of 'Fiddler on the Roof' at a local high school. Having three daughters, and being someone who loves tradition, it's one of my favourite movies. We spent half the ride home deciding which of Tevye's daughters is most like Amy and her sisters.

"I've started to tithe," she told me as we turned into the driveway.

"Your dad set the example for you just like Grandpa did for me. Having a Christian heritage is something to be thankful for."

"I'm reading Proverbs again," she said. "It's so full of wisdom."

"Really?" She catches the tone in my voice and laughs.

The memories of these times we spend together are carefully stored in my heart like the mementoes from special events stored in my Memory Box.

A few days later, I felt like I'd been run over by a bus. I rarely spent a day in bed, but my head was pounding and every inch of my body ached. Bouts of nausea interrupted the sweet sleep of oblivion. When I heard Amy on the phone making plans to go out, I wanted to tell her not to drive tonight, to get one of her friends to pick her up instead. It didn't make sense. There was no real sense of danger, just a feeling—a feeling that wouldn't go away.

I heard the sound of her tires crunching through the snow as she left and pushed aside the nagging thought that I should have followed my intuition and talked to her. Throughout the night, I woke up several times feeling an urgency to pray for Amy's safety. I reminded myself that she was in the safest place she could be—in God's hands.

Bill was up early the next morning, getting ready to go to church. My aching body told me I'd be spending another day in bed. The slam of a car door in the driveway caught my attention. Amy was home. It surprised me to hear her saying good-bye to someone. I asked my husband about it and soon heard his raised voice and her sobs in the hallway.

Fear prickled up my spine and constricted my throat. When they came into the bedroom, I could tell by her face that something terrible had happened. The story came out in halting words between sobs. She had been at a bar drinking. Her friend wanted cigarettes.

"I always call a cab," she said, her voice hoarse from crying.

But not tonight. Tonight she drove and collided with a cab.

I couldn't bear to hear any more. I wanted to put my hands over my ears and stop her words—words that stabbed my heart like poisoned darts. *Is she completely irresponsible? This can't be my daughter speaking.* She continued with her story. When the police came, she blew over the limit. The officer charged her and took her to jail.

"I'll have a criminal record," she said, wiping her nose on her sleeve, but she couldn't wipe the misery from her face. I felt the paralyzing effects of the darts, and heard the mocking laughter of the enemy. *I've won! I am victorious!*

She knelt by the bed, begging for forgiveness and vowing she would never drink again. I was stunned. I couldn't speak. Bill put his arms around her. "There is nothing you could ever do that would make us stop loving you." He pulled both of us into a hug and together we prayed for our humiliated daughter.

Amy

It was 4:30 a.m. Sunday morning. I was sitting alone in a jail cell with empty pockets, no shoes, no jewelry, and no belt. I didn't know how many hours had passed since the police officer locked me in. When I told him I needed to use the washroom he just raised his eyebrows and smiled. He motioned with a tip of his head to an open toilet on the other wall, "Please do," he said. *Thanks, but no thanks,* I thought to myself when I walked in.

But now after hours had passed I had no choice. I un-buttoned my pants as fast as I could. My hands and legs trembled as I tried to squat above the toilet. Pulling my shirt as low as I could to cover myself, I felt a single tear roll down my cheek. I sat back down on the cold cot hugging my knees with my back to the camera. Scared and disgusted with myself, it felt like an eternity had passed. I hated the quietness. Being left alone with my tormenting thoughts disgusted me.

All that was going through my mind was "Cut the strings and be free, Amy", familiar words that I'd heard time and time again in my prayers. "Cut the strings and be free, be free of the things that chain you to sin, be free of the things that hold you captive. Be free!" As I sat trying to change my thoughts it occurred to me that maybe, just maybe, God was trying to tell me something. Since there isn't much else to do alone in a 4 by 4 foot jail cell, I finally decided to listen. For years I'd ignored his voice, pretended I didn't hear it, and even not believed it. But it's when I actually listened to it that good things began to happen in my life!

It seemed like a regular night out. We had been at the pub most of the night drinking double rye and coke. I was always one to order the strong drinks, drinking them without flinching somehow made me feel tough. As I pounded back drink after drink, I said to Jen that we should take a cab home, since neither one of us was stopping any time soon. *Odd . . . I thought to myself . . . I've never mentioned getting a cab any other night, since it was usually a given that I would drive.* For some reason tonight seemed different. I was aware of something, something in the back of my mind, something I couldn't quite put my finger on.

The night lingered on and the pub was closing. As we walked out of the bar I saw my car parked across the street and the thought of getting a cab immediately left my mind. We climbed in, cranked the tunes and headed out. I needed smokes so the convenience store was the first stop, but as we pulled out there was a horrific noise.

A cab slammed into the driver's side of my car and it spun round. The sound of twisting metal and tires squealing sent people running for help. I sat in a daze. It had seemed to me that the cab was miles away. How could he have smashed into us? Where did he come from? My mind was a blur. Stepping on the gas I tried to get away, but the car wouldn't move. *There's no point in running now,* I thought to myself. Trying to get out I pushed hard with my shoulder on the door. It was no use, the door was crushed in. I crawled across the seat and Jen helped me out. As we sat down on the curb the taxi driver yelled and swore at me. Oddly I said nothing. My mind was on something else. *Did I really hear that? "I've cut the strings"* or was I imagining it? I swore that an almost audible voice had said it just before we crashed.

My head lifted as I heard the police sirens in the distance. Jen came out of the convenience store with a coffee for me. I wrapped my hands around the warm cup and stood up. I knew that there would be no talking my way out of this one.

I'd been in other accidents before, even been pulled over several times, and was always able to make up a convincing story that somehow got me off the hook. I would usually smile sweetly and talk my way out of trouble. This time I had nothing to say. Did I want to be caught? Did I want to be done with it all?

After I told the police officer what happened he escorted me to the cruiser. I walked quietly behind him, my feet slowly shuffling along. The happiness from my double ryes had left me. It was just me and reality now. I blew hard into the breathalyzer, knowing what the outcome would be. I turned to face the cop car. Grabbing my hands behind my back the officer cuffed me. I stood there feeling no surprise, no shock, and no outrage. I knew this was what I deserved.

It felt like a long ride to police station. While the cops laughed and talked up front I sat quietly in the back. *Odd, I thought to myself. Just a few weeks ago I was at the front of our church giving my life to you, Lord. Now I'm cuffed in the back of a cruiser. Why couldn't I have stopped before it came to this? Why didn't I cut the strings?*

TWENTY NINE

WHAT DO WE DO NOW, LORD?

Sharon

The bottom fell out of our world. It felt as if I were sliding down a long black tunnel into desperation. Only a few months after Amy committed her life to Christ, she plunged right back into the life she knew so well. She wasn't talking much, but what she did say broke my heart. We heard more details—none of them good.

After the accident, the police officer tested her and placed her under arrest. Amy was taken to the station where she spent several hours in a jail cell. When she asked to use the bathroom, an officer told her to use the one in the cell. She told me it was totally degrading trying to cover herself as much as possible in open view of all who passed by and with a video camera on her. She felt completely humiliated.

Today I tried to process the information. The ramifications of her decision last night turned the muscles in my shoulders into knots of stone, adding to the discomfort I felt from the flu.

Amy looked ill and I wondered if she was suffering from a hang over or from guilt.

I thought of what Joseph said to his brothers, "You intended to harm me, but God intended it for good…"[32] I believed the enemy wanted to use this accident to bring about Amy's downfall, the thing that would make her feel completely worthless and cause her to walk away from God and never come back. I knew God had a different plan in mind. Somehow he would bring good out of this calamity, but at this point, I couldn't see how.

Her car had to be towed to a storage lot. Without wheels, she was house-bound. Not that she could drive anywhere. She auto-matically lost her licence for three months when they charged her. The phone remained strangely quiet. Her life-long friends seemed to have vanished.

When our pastor called, she refused to come to the phone. I encouraged her to talk to him. I knew he would understand. She dragged herself to the phone. The few words she spoke were forced through lips that refused to share her shame.

With tears in her eyes, she said Pastor Frank had told her about an incident in his own life that happened after he had accepted Christ. He knew how she felt. He encouraged her and told her he'd be praying for her. She admitted she didn't feel so alone.

Journal Entry: January 20, 2004

Even before I opened my eyes this morning, my mind recalled verses I had read many times. "And my God will meet all your needs according to his glorious riches in Christ Jesus,"[33] and "Trust in the LORD with all your heart and lean not on your own understanding; in all your ways acknowledge him, and he will make your paths straight."[34] I wrote out the verses and taped them to the bathroom mirror. We will need these reminders of his daily care many times as we walk through the next few days. I added this quote that challenged me to keep my focus on God: "We shall steer safely through every storm, so long as our heart is right, our intention fervent, our courage steadfast, and our trust fixed on God." Saint Francis de Sales

My husband and I worked out a schedule to drive Amy to work and pick her up. On the days I drove we sometimes talked, and other times the only sound in the car was the music from the radio. My emotions were as raw as scraped skin. I didn't know what her thoughts were, but mine were consumed with trying to understand the increasing distance between us. Three months ago, she had genuinely committed her life to Christ. Now, she could be facing a jail term. Turmoil filled my mind as I drove home. *I don't understand. I don't know what to do.*

When I got home I noticed that the house needed a good cleaning. As I walked past Amy's bedroom, a thought penetrated my anxious mind with startling force. *I am calling you to love Amy, not only with words, but with actions. Love her unconditionally, as I love her. Unconditionally, the way I love you. Clean her room as an act of love.* I recognized God's prompting. *Am I hearing you right, Lord? Is this really what you want me to do? Clean her room?*

Her messy room had always been a bone of contention between us. I saw it as part of my house and therefore felt it should be kept clean and tidy at all times. She saw it as her personal space, her private world, and felt that keeping the door shut was a workable solution. I sensed this was God's way of showing me something important in these dark days so I threw myself into the challenge. It took several hours to gather the laundry, put fresh sheets on the bed, vacuum and dust. I hadn't seen the floor of this room for some time.

I bought a small plant, put it in a colourful pot and placed a little note beside it. It explained how we need to stay rooted in God, and how he tenderly cares for us every day, producing new life and growth in our lives, transforming us more and more into the likeness of his Son. I understood that loving her the way God loves her did not mean condoning her sinful lifestyle any more than his love for me condones my sin.

The decision to go to Son-Up this morning left me feeling guilty. I didn't want to face the ladies in the Bible study at our church, but I'd made a commitment to lead a discussion group. On one hand, I knew that if I talked to anyone, I'd burst into tears, yet being there gave me a much needed reprieve—a few hours to allow my mind to rest.

Several ladies noticed the strain on my face and asked if anything was wrong. Their sincere concern for me showed on their faces. I ached to talk with someone, but I felt the information was Amy's and not mine to share. My pride kept me from reaching out for the help I needed. Why couldn't I just be honest? Why couldn't I tell someone it felt as if we were walking in a deep valley with huge mountains on either side, blocking out the sunlight? Why couldn't I admit that I needed a shoulder to cry on?

To be honest, I would have been embarrassed if they found out what was happening to our daughter. What would they think of me as a mother? Of us as Christian parents? Amy walked down the aisle and committed her life to Christ and look where she ended up a few months later.

In our discussion groups women sometimes shared their journeys of faith when dealing with their rebellious teenagers. I didn't want to fall into the trap of assuming God wanted me to deal with my daughter in exactly the same way. There were days when I felt desperate enough to do just that—take what worked for someone else and apply it to Amy—at least I would be doing something. But in my heart I knew my answers would only come as I waited patiently before God.

In this process I'd heard a lot of advice but I learned that God does not give out cookie-cutter direction. He knows us intimately and deals with us individually. When I spent time on my knees earnestly praying, he gave wisdom and guidance for each situation and enough strength to face each day.

The undercurrent of tension intensified in our home. It felt like a living thing. Amy stayed in her room, cutting herself off from the family. Once in a while a new piece of information surfaced. It seemed she couldn't say it all at once. Her whole demeanor screamed hopelessness.

We asked her what she wanted to do, but she seemed incapable of making decisions. We assured her that we would support whatever she decided. We were all in this together because we are a family, but ultimately in the end, she would have to face the consequences herself. I spent hours on the phone trying to get information to at least give her some options. Should we approach Legal Aid? Or P.O.I.N.T.S.? *Did she need a lawyer?* I wondered.

Amy was adamant that she must pay the penalty for her actions. She would willingly pay a fine, go to jail, or do both, whatever the judge ruled. She planned to throw herself on the mercy of the court. When someone suggested that she would be considered innocent until the court proved her guilty, she protested, "But I'm not innocent, and I deserve whatever I get."

I asked if she wanted me to make some calls, and she agreed. Working two jobs gave her little time to contact anyone during office hours. The following day, I made my first call to Legal Aid. Never in my wildest dreams did I ever think I'd be going down this road. After explaining the circumstances, the receptionist told me that Legal Aid did not handle criminal cases. Just hearing the word—criminal—broke my heart.

I had seen ads for P.O.I.N.T.S. on television. When I called the office, I quickly discovered they didn't handle any case where alcohol is involved. As I hung up the phone, I realized that in the space of eight minutes, the two avenues of help I'd counted on were gone. *Lord, where do we turn now? What's the next step?*

The stress affected all of us. I could see it clearly on Bill's face. Our finances were already strained. I tried to hide my tears, but I couldn't stop their flow. I cried out to God for wisdom and direction. Sometimes I felt his presence and his peace. At other times, I felt nothing. I fought the fears that hounded me like a menacing dog, seemingly alone.

With all that was happening I found it difficult to concentrate on writing. The deadline for the devotionals was a few weeks away. I had to honour the contract I signed.

The tedious process of editing and rewriting sapped what little energy I had left. In light of what we were going through I felt I had gained some new insights, but I sat and stared at the computer screen, unable to write. My mind whirled with words and phrases like butterflies fluttering just out of reach. "I can't do it! I'll never make the deadline," I shouted at the screen. Panic set in.

The few sentences I managed to write lay on the page, pale and weak. The room felt dark even though sunlight streamed through the window. Discouragement settled in like an uninvited guest. How did I ever come to believe that I was a writer? The tears flowed again as I pressed delete and my feeble attempts vanished from the screen.

On Friday morning, when Amy came home for lunch, my husband suggested we call our lawyer to get some facts and a recommendation for a criminal lawyer if she decided to go that route. Amy and I were both on the phone. What we heard left us numb.

She could be fined $500–$600; need a $1500 retainer; pay $4,000 more if her case went to trial; could lose her licence for up to two years; pay $500. to take an alcohol-education course to get her licence back; pay $1500 for an ignition interlock system installed in any car she owned or operated. This device insured that the car wouldn't start without her breathing into it and registering an acceptable blood-alcohol level.

What about insurance? Would any company insure her now? I thought. Does she need a lawyer? That's the question we were all asking. Could she go to court on her own? If she did, she would be given a court-appointed lawyer. These lawyers probably handled hundreds of cases. How much would he do for her case? We needed answers. No one seemed to have any.

THIRTY

BEAUTY FROM ASHES

Amy
Journal Entry: January 23, 2004

So what's left? What's left when you can't point to anything in your life with pride? What's left when I've become everything I hate? What was going through my head? How and why did all these things I used to be so opposed to have such a grip on my life? Was it a weakening? Did I weaken my morals until I had none? What a waste! What a hole I've dug for myself. Why couldn't I open my eyes and see what I've done to my life? I guess I was just wingin' it? Nothing had killed me yet, although some had come close. The strong willed, intelligent, moral person I was . . . where did she go?

Anyway that's the past, and if there's one good thing about it, it's that it is over. How do you live with yourself after this? How do I live with myself? I suppose the same way everyone else does, they move on. I've been so lucky with my life. I couldn't ask for better parents, they don't deserve a daughter like me. They love me, they discipline me, they teach me, and they listen to me. There is nothing I could ask of my parents that they haven't already given to me. They don't deserve a daughter like me. If I could only turn back time. What a mess I've made. Forgive me, forgive me.

But anyway, that's enough complaining about me. It's not about what I've done, it's about what I'm going to do. Right! What am I going to do? What the hell am I going to do? Gave up hard drugs two months ago, gave up weed one month ago, and gave up alcohol six days ago. Well, it's not much but I guess it's a start. God, help me, six days totally sober and counting!

Sharon

At my lowest point today my good friend Linda called. I couldn't hold back the tears while I told her I was having trouble getting my assignment finished. I wanted to share with her what we were going through, but felt I couldn't burden her with our problems with what she faced.

Linda had been diagnosed with cancer and was bravely fighting her own battle. Her smile, positive attitude and indomitable spirit inspired all who knew her. She walked closely with her Lord, trusting him completely and holding his hand as she faced difficult days with the calm assurance of his presence.

She must have heard something in my voice because she immediately asked what else was wrong. Without giving many details, I simply asked Linda to remember our family in prayer. After she prayed with me, she asked if it would help to have her edit my devotionals. Putting aside her own health concerns, she generously offered her time, energy and skills. What an example of a servant's heart. I gratefully accepted.

On Sunday morning, I wondered if Amy would go with us to church. All week she kept repeating how ashamed she felt. She didn't know if she had the courage to face the people at church. In a city this size, news travels fast.

It surprised me to hear her say, "I have to go. I'm going. It's the right thing to do."

We sat in our usual spot. It's funny how one gets comfortable in a certain pew. Our pastor's wife, Maureen, commented that many people are in the same seat every Sunday morning. It made it easier to take attendance during the service.

I sang the familiar worship choruses with little enthusiasm. The words rolled off my tongue, but my soul felt shriveled and dry. When it came time to shake hands and welcome each other, Amy stayed in her seat, trying to remain as inconspicuous as possible in our large congregation. I noticed Pastor Frank leave the platform. I watched as he walked all the way over to the other side of the room and gave Amy a hug. That action spoke volumes—not only to her, but to us. He is a wise, caring and compassionate man of God who has a shepherd's heart for his congregation and for our city.

I woke up Monday morning feeling emotionally exhausted. I found it hard to concentrate let alone pray. When I needed it most, I let my worries crowd out my time with God. I realized that my frustrations stemmed from my assumption that all of Amy's addictions would disappear the moment she committed her life to Christ. We had ample proof that they hadn't.

I felt like a yoyo. Some days full of faith and eager to see what God would do next, and other times failing, falling back into unbelief, desperate to hear from God yet not hearing his gentle voice. *What am I missing in all of this, Lord? I know you have things to teach each of us through this. Where is your answer today?*

Two things stood in opposition: What I wanted to be true and what I knew to be true from the Scriptures. I had to remind myself that Amy was in a process. Yes, sometimes God removes the appetite that keeps a person in bondage. More often, he walks with us through our recovery, helping us up each time we fall. Our will must come into line with his, and we must find our strength in him alone. Our ability and strength will fail us every time.

We found out today that Amy might be able to plead to a lesser charge of careless driving. We may need a lawyer after all because she cannot get her police report until she retains a lawyer. Just when I thought there couldn't be more bad news.

Whispering a prayer for guidance, I opened the phone book. Over my 46 years of walking with God, I am still discovering the wonderful ways he directs our paths and gives us wisdom when we ask him.

The very first ad I noticed stated in bold letters "IMPAIRED CHARGE. Need your licence? There is HOPE!" What a welcome word. Hope. As I bowed my head in thanksgiving, I realized afresh that no matter what help this lawyer could give us, our hope was anchored in God. He would direct us, and give us peace in the turmoil.

Later that day when Amy called the office, she was impressed with the professional way she was treated. She made the decision to retain the services of a defence lawyer from that firm. The initial consultation will be $500. She will have to pay $4000–$5000. more if the case goes to court.

I was still torn over Amy's decision. *Should she have left it all in God's hands? Was her decision to retain a lawyer the right one?* The choice must be Amy's since she was the one facing a criminal charge. We had prayed earnestly and faithfully that God would give us his answer. Now, I *had* to believe he did and that this was part of his plan.

Amy
Journal Entry: January 28, 2004

We may think we're happy but we're not. This world is like a plague, a plague that causes depression, hatred, envy and greed, continually producing ugly deadly sin. If only the people of the world would turn their eyes to Jesus, their loving Savior. But they can not. The world is burning with lust for itself, lost in the darkness of its sin. I spent too many years in the darkness of my sin, listening to the voice that was coaxing me on. The world is full of tempting, teasing, pleasurable things. But you can't run from the light forever. We all know, everyone of us knows, we are guilty. We try so many things to cover up that guilt.

Jesus just wants us to be free. He wants us to come to him, so he can set us free from the chains we forge. Everything has its price, most are impossible to pay. There is One who has paid our bill for us, if only we would come to him. He stands with arms outstretched in love ready to wipe our slate clean. He is gentle, he is patient, and he is love.

Jesus gives purpose to a meaningless drifter. Jesus and only Jesus is freedom. This has nothing to do with what we've done or who we are. It has everything to with what Jesus did on the cross, and who he is. If you think you can find hope, peace or freedom from this world you are sadly mistaken. Look around at the world, it cannot offer you any of those things. This world and everything in it is temporary, all it has to offer us is temporary fixes. Everything eternal and lasting comes from God. He brings understanding, peace, joy and hope. Without him life has no meaning. Come to him and find purpose. Come to him and find love. Come to him and find forgiveness. But do not expect the world to understand.

THIRTY ONE

A TEST OF FAITH

Sharon

God blessed me in wonderful ways through a group of women who knew how to pray and how to love. There were seven of us, including my mentor, Linda, who met twice a month to pray together for a greater outpouring of God's Holy Spirit in our own lives and in our church. We shared prayer requests and praise reports. Often, with arms around each other, we prayed for our families. The bond that united us went far deeper than friendship. We were sisters bound together by God's love first and foremost.

We have prayed and wept with each other, laughed together, found answers in God's Word together, counseled and encouraged each other, taken phone calls at any time of the day or night, and have always sought to point each other to Christ at all times, and in all circumstances. I treasured the relationship I had with these wonderful women of God.

Prior to our meeting that week, I asked Amy's permission to share the details of what happened on the night of her accident.

The group had been praying for our daughter over the past few years and that night, when I shared my heart with them, they immediately gathered around me to pray. In the days to come, their prayer support helped to keep me strong as the winds and waves of the storm raged against our family.

I gradually shared more and more of what was happening to Amy with our church family and experienced an outpouring of compassion, and encouragement—priceless gifts. I have to admit I have always felt more comfortable giving than receiving, but being the recipient of such genuine love, the kind of love that sees beyond all your faults and chooses to stand by your side, is the greatest gift one could ever receive.

When I asked for prayer, there were some who told me they had received a word from the Lord for me. I listened carefully and then checked to see if it agreed with Scripture —the plumb line of Truth. I invited the Holy Spirit to bring my life in line with his Truth, and watched for confirmation through trustworthy followers of Christ. My husband, Bill, often encouraged me when my faith faltered, and I tried to do the same for him. Through 33 years of marriage we have weathered many storms together, not always well, but always with a heart that wanted above all to please God.

During this time, our church was involved in a building program called Growing Together. We were challenged to pray and obey; pray and ask God for the amount he would have us give, and give it over a period of three years. One morning, during my prayer time God brought a certain figure to my mind. The amount astonished me. Perhaps it wasn't God, I reasoned, but deep down I knew the impression came from him.

When I shared what I felt God had spoken to me with my husband, who had also been praying, he looked surprised.

"God hasn't shown me a specific amount," he said. "But if this is what God wants us to do, then we will pledge that amount and trust him to provide." And with that the matter was settled, though I couldn't see how we could possibly give this money above our weekly tithes and offerings. It would be a real test of faith for me.

Growing up with my three siblings, our parents taught us to pray and trust God to provide for our needs. I saw God answer those prayers in miraculous ways. After Bill and I were married, a fear in the area of finances began to take root in my life. Even with the rich legacy of God's faithfulness, I began to equate security with the balance in our bank book. God was about to challenge that lie.

As I prayed about it over the next few weeks, I began to feel the stirrings of excitement about what God would teach us through this process. He impressed upon my heart that taking this step of faith would break the bondage of fear that finances held over my life. My husband and I held hands and committed ourselves and our money to God.

"No matter what we have to do, we are going to meet our pledge," he said.

We started when our children were young to teach them that we would always be there to support them, but not to pay their way through life. We wanted them to learn to take responsibility. Amy told us up front that whatever we had to pay out now to help her with lawyer and court costs, she would pay us back in full. We believed her.

The strain of what she faced had an effect on our whole family. Julie and Michelle found ways to let her know they were there for her. Michelle often talked with Amy and shared what

God had done in her life, encouraging her not to give up when she failed.

Julie found practical ways to show support for her sister by offering to drive Amy to the animal hospital where she worked. She often stayed to help her with the cleaning. The fact that Amy mentioned it more than once told me it touched her heart. Acts of kindness speak louder than words. Knowing that your family loves you no matter what you do is amazing. It's what our heavenly Father does for us.

When Julie decided to make a bedroom for Amy in her spacious laundry room, as a surprise, we all got involved in the plan. One Saturday afternoon while Amy was at work, we transformed an ordinary laundry room into a home away from home. Pretty curtains were hung to create a private space and pictures adorned the walls. An alarm clock, a scented candle and a lamp were arranged on a bed-side table. A pretty basket held a pair of fluffy slippers, and a cozy bathrobe lay across the end of the bed.

That night, after work, Amy arrived and saw the room all prepared for her. She was overwhelmed. "You can stay here whenever you want to," Julie told her. "It will give you a break from being at home with Mom and Dad." Amy laughed at that remark. What fun we had showering her with love.

With the whole family gathered together, we decided to order pizza and make it a celebration. Our lost sheep had come home and all the sheep in her family were doing their best to make her feel loved and accepted.

What will our reaction be, I wondered, when we see for the first time what God has prepared in heaven for those who love him—sinners saved by his grace? I believe we will be awe-struck.

THIRTY TWO

TRUSTING GOD IN THE DARK

Sharon

The blustery month of January eased into a snowy February. Amy met with her lawyer for the first time on Sunday, February 1, 2004. She and her dad left part way through the service to make it in time for the 11:30 appointment.

I have always loved gathering together with the family of God on Sundays. Now, it had become an oasis for me. The atmosphere of praise and worship calmed my mind, and refreshed my spirit. Hearing reports of the good things God was doing in our church family and all over the world assured me once again that the same God was watching over all of us. That Sunday, Pastor Frank preached on "Facing Down Fear"—a timely message for me.

The following morning, I thought about the outcome of Amy's appointment with renewed hope. According to her lawyer the fact that she hadn't been charged with impairment was in her favour. With my limited knowledge of court proceedings, I didn't know how much weight that would carry with the judge.

Throughout the day I found it hard to focus on anything but what was happening to our family. The thought of Amy sitting in a jail cell brought tears to my eyes. My stomach churned with worry. I wrestled with the fear that she might turn away from God.

I couldn't stop the terrible scenarios that played out in my mind. Once more fear tracked me like a black shadow. I felt its ominous presence. *God, you have freed me from some of my worst fears. Why do I feel like I'm slipping down a long slope only to end up right back where I was before?*

Resist the devil, and he will flee from you,[35] came God's answer. The words echoed in my head, arresting my attention like an order from a commanding officer. I realized this was an attack of the enemy, an assault meant to enslave me again, and God was telling me how to defeat him.

As I sat at my computer, intending to finish a project, the lines of a poem began forming in my mind. I typed them as I experienced them.

Intruder

> He stood before me
> Tall and threatening,
> His eyes aflame with self-importance,
> His presence filling every inch of the room.
> I sank helplessly into a chair.
> He ordered me to stand.
> Trembling, I obeyed,
> All the time wondering
> How he came to be in my room.

"I've come to tell you
Your situation is hopeless."
His lips curled into a sneer.
"No one can help you."
He laid a heavy hand on my shoulder.
I bowed my head in despair.
"What can I do?" I moaned.
"Do!" he shouted.
"There is nothing you can do!"
Then bending close to my ear,
So close I could feel his breath upon my neck,
He whispered, "You are a failure.
No one cares for you."
I sank to my knees sobbing.
His words stung my heart.
All that I feared was true.
I had no defence against his absolute authority.
He turned to leave, his black coat
Brushing against my tear stained face.
"Wait," I gasped. "I must know your name."
His evil laugh echoed off the walls.
"I am FEAR. I rule minds."
I heard it then—
An almost undetectable hesitation
In his arrogant declaration.
And I knew the truth.
He had no control
Only what I had given him.
The lie was his.
The choice was mine.

I began to understand how this attempt to sabotage my faith had kept me distracted and unable to finish the devotionals I'd promised to write. Interestingly, the one I had begun that day was titled: Faith or Fear. I would write them now with a new perspective.

On Wednesday, Bill took Amy to the Police Station to be fingerprinted and have her booking photograph taken. I couldn't go with them. I couldn't watch an officer snap a mug shot of my daughter. I didn't want that memory stamped on my mind. Her records will be on file and available for every police force to see. She now has a criminal record. My grip was tenuous as I clung to the illusion that this really couldn't be happening to our family.

After several more appointments with her lawyer, Amy had her first court appearance. Waiting at home I prayed for the judge who would hear her case. I didn't know his name, but God did. I prayed that he would be used of God no matter what decision he made.

"I had to sit through ten other cases," Amy told me when she got home. "I got a real good look at how my life could have ended up and the consequences of the life I'd been living. I didn't have to say anything. My lawyer asked for an adjournment and the judge agreed. All I need to do now is to get a copy of the disclosure from the lawyer."

The day we got the police report, we sat at the kitchen table and read it together. Visibly upset, Amy pointed out all the lies, especially the long list of witnesses on the cabby's side. "When will I get to tell my side of the story to the District Attorney?" she asked. Her voice betrayed her fear. I looked at her face and wondered, *how did we ever end up here?*

"Let's pray and ask God to go before you and make a way for the truth to be heard," I suggested, feeling faith rise up within me. We held hands and prayed that she would have God's wisdom for every decision and that she would trust him completely with her life—whatever the outcome might be.

I still felt plagued by "what-ifs" but I found I could more quickly roll them onto God's shoulders, and feel the freedom of knowing he would take care of everything that concerned us. I taped another verse to our bathroom mirror. It gave me renewed courage. "I know that you can do all things; no plan of yours can be thwarted." Job 42:2

The strain showed on our faces as we tried to maintain a normal life. Bill found it harder to deal with because he went with Amy to all of her appointments, each one a painful reminder of how far our daughter had fallen. Every day, we renewed our hope as we proclaimed again, "Jesus is Amy's Advocate." We were all learning in our own way to trust through this painful process. I've heard it said, "Trust grows in the darkness when we can't see the light." God knows how to shine his light in the darkest places.

Amy came home from her next appointment with some good news. She was surprised when her lawyer immediately asked what things in the police report weren't true. "He thinks he can get the charges dropped to careless driving. I'll lose some demerit points, but I won't have a criminal record," she told me, her voice sounding hopeful.

As I drove her to work the next morning, she cranked up the volume on the radio and we sang, He Reigns, along with the Newsboys at the top of our lungs. I looked at her and laughed. I loved having my daughter back.

"When I gave my heart to God, I really gave him everything. I want to serve him, and only him. I'll never drink again. He showed me what a fake I was, living that other life." Her voice broke with emotion. "I don't care if I have to go to jail. I know I'm forgiven, and I'm willing to pay the penalty."

When I got home, I checked the calendar to see when Amy had her next appointment with her lawyer and saw the notation on Sunday March 14. As I looked at the date, I realized that three years ago in March we were helping her move into an apartment. So much had happened in that time. Now she was a new woman in Christ, facing an unknown future.

I read again the verse Bill felt impressed to give her yesterday. "The LORD is good to those whose hope is in him, to the one who seeks him; it is good to wait quietly for the salvation of the LORD."[36] Hoping and waiting—that's what we were doing.

PEACE OF MIND

Sharon

Amy said she wanted to talk to us tonight. I immediately thought she had heard from her lawyer. One look at her face told me it wasn't good news.

"I don't know how to say this." She paused as if she were searching for the right words.

"Just say it. You know there isn't anything we can't talk about. We've already been through a lot together."

"I . . . I was . . . pregnant . . . at the same time as Julie . . . " Her voice trailed off. My husband and I sat in stunned silence. The ticking of the clock sounded like a gong in the room.

"It was hard for me to watch her with her newborn baby . . . to see all the happiness it brought you and Dad. I wanted to tell you then, but . . . but I just couldn't get the words out." She paused again and reached for a tissue. "I felt so ashamed because I knew deep down what I did was horribly wrong. I'd listened to the enemy's lies for so long they actually made sense."

I moved to sit close to her and put my arm around her shoulders. We waited for her to go on.

"I've asked God to forgive me, but I'm not sure I can ever forgive myself. I've been thinking about volunteering at the Pregnancy Crisis Center. I'd share my story if I can help one woman choose to keep her baby . . . " She couldn't go on.

"Were you pregnant the Christmas when you were so sick?" I asked, wiping the tears from my eyes.

"Yes, I was throwing up so much I got scared."

"Honey, why couldn't you come to us? You know we would have helped you keep your baby, helped you in whatever way you needed. Done anything . . . " My words were infused with pain, a terrible searing pain that tore at my heart as I thought of the loss of a precious tiny life.

Bill had quietly listened with tears in his eyes while Amy cried, reliving her horrendous experience. He left his chair and came to sit beside her on the couch.

"We need to pray about this," he said. "The enemy has stolen enough from us." As he prayed, asking God to forgive us as parents for the times we had failed our daughter, I was never so proud of my husband. He prayed that Amy would experience and accept God's forgiveness and allow his healing to remove the crushing weight of guilt and shame she felt.

A tangible awareness of God's presence filled the room. I believe the healing started as we held each other close and continued to pray.

Journal Entry: February 20, 2004

When a tsunami hits you there is seldom any warning. Its effects are devastating. Today Amy told us she had an abortion.

It's hard to write these words. Tears are dropping on the pages. My thoughts are fragmented.

My darling daughter, what pain you must have endured. How lost you must have felt. What a devastating experience to go through alone, yet not alone. God was with you, crying for you. Crying for his lost, hurting child. Wanting you to know he still loves you. He has never stopped loving you.

I wonder, was your baby a boy or a girl? What colour eyes? What colour hair?

My arms ache to hold this precious child who would have been our grandbaby. I believe this little one is in heaven with Jesus. One day, we'll all be together, our whole family, in the presence of God. Perhaps Mom is holding your sweet baby in her arms while Jesus whispers softly, "I love you. Welcome home, little one."

Father, please hold Amy in your arms tonight and for the rest of her life. Assure her that nothing she has done or will ever do will make you stop loving her. When she cries alone, remind her that you see every one of her tears.

Tomorrow I'll share this verse of Scripture with her. "You have seen me tossing and turning through the night. You have collected all my tears and preserved them in your bottle! You have recorded every one in your book."[37] It will bring healing and comfort to both of us.

Amy
Journal Entry: February 21, 2004

Today you taught me something new, Lord!! What it means to be real, open and honest. Not to hide or change myself for others. Forgive me Lord, forgive me. It was you that I was hiding; it was Jesus in my life that I was hiding from everyone. How horribly stupid of me! You are who I am! If only we could all see ourselves just as you see us God, as your beautiful sons and daughters perfectly created by your hand. Each one of us has immeasurable value, purpose and beauty.

Even when I was drinking and using drugs I was just suppressing and fighting who I was. In my deepest heart I yearned for God. It was tearing me apart! I was unsure of everything about myself. I was anxious, hopeless and so tired of the fight that raged inside of me! Drugs and alcohol took over my troubled mind. It was easier to get instant gratification and pleasure than it was to deal with the reality of what I had become.

Jesus you were lovingly knocking on the door of my heart. I denied it but heard it loud and clear. You knocked louder, harder. I drank more, I used more. You stopped knocking, sat down in front of the door and waited. Finally I let you in. Thank you, thank you for not leaving! I will no longer dismiss you for anyone. I will no longer hide the only good thing about me. I do, and always have believed in you. I will no longer deny you and live in turmoil. Instead I will embrace you and live in peace of mind. At last, peace of mind!

Sharon

I sat in church nervously waiting for Bill and Amy and to return from her appointment, wondering what news there might be. As the service began, I prayed for God's mercy. I couldn't stand the thought of Amy sitting in a jail cell after what she told us about the night of the accident, but I knew she would have to pay for her offense.

As I sang the worship chorus, Blessed Be Your Name, the words took on new meaning for me. *On the road marked with suffering, though there's pain in the offering, blessed be Your name.'* We were walking that road. *'When the darkness closes in, Lord, still I will say, blessed be the name of the Lord.'* I had experienced that darkness. *"You give and take away, You give and take away, my heart will choose to say, Lord, blessed be Your name.'*[38] We didn't know what the future held, but we had made our choice. We would trust God and face the future unafraid.

When Amy and Bill slipped into the seat beside me I couldn't tell by their expressions if the news had been good or bad.

"What happened? I want to know every detail," I insisted as we walked to the car.

"We'll discuss it when we get home," Bill said. That convinced me things hadn't gone well. He seemed to deliberately drive slower than usual. It was the longest six kilometer drive in history. Nobody spoke a word. *What did her lawyer say to have them react like this?* I wondered.

The instant we got inside the door, the look of gloom dropped from their faces.

"The lawyer told us he was flabbergasted. That was his exact word. Flabbergasted! He's handled hundreds of cases like Amy's and has 140 similar cases right now, but he has *never* seen this happen before." Bill stopped for a breath. "He said this particular judge always demands his pound of flesh in cases like this. He never lets anyone with alcohol related charges off the hook."

Amy took over the story. "My lawyer said the results were far better than he'd hoped for. All the charges were dropped, and my record is cleared. I'll have my licence back in ninety days from the time of the accident."

"That's it?" I asked, hardly able to take it all in.

"I have to take an alcohol-education course in Lindsay and attend five Alcoholics Anonymous meetings," she added. "I'll only have my lawyer's fee and the course to pay for."

"And her lawyer agreed to deal with the insurance company for us," Bill added. His face looked younger than it had in years.

I sat at the kitchen table hardly able to absorb what they said. Flabbergasted! Astounded! That's what I felt. No trial, no jail time, no fine, no interlock system in her car, no careless driving charge. To me it was a miracle—something only God could accomplish. A judge changing his well-established pattern of sentencing—unbelievable.

God allowed the accident to happen and used it as a tool to work in Amy's life, but he alone controlled the entire outcome! Only he could change the minds of those involved. I suddenly remembered one of the Scripture verses I'd clung to all through this journey. Proverbs 13:12. "Delayed hope makes the heart sick; but when dreams come true at last, there is life and joy." We had been living with delayed hope all this time, now we were celebrating life and joy!

I was speechless—and for me, that's something.

Amy
Journal Entry: March 9, 2004

Wow! What an amazing, merciful, wonderful God!! Dad and I went to the lawyer to hear the outcome of my charges today . . . NOTHING!! I'm charged with nothing! Not over 80. Not careless driving. It's unbelievable. The lawyer said he's never seen anything like it! I guess I'm still in shock. I thought at best I would get careless driving charges; the worst, jail time. It was enough for me Lord that you forgave me, I needed nothing else. God in all his glory has set me free of everything! What a merciful, merciful God. He's given me a clean slate, a fresh start.

I'll stop destroying my life with drugs and alcohol and give it back to God because he has proven to me that he can do amazing things with my life! What I've done in my life is sinful and horribly wrong, but now you Lord have turned my life into something good! I am so undeserving and always will be, nothing can change that. All I can do is what you have called me to do: serve God with all my heart, all my mind, all my soul! Praise be to God who has lovingly welcomed back a lost little girl. He has given me a second chance, and with that I will serve Him!

EPILOGUE

SHARON

During the months of April and May, Amy completed the alcohol-education course and the required AA meetings. When Bill drove her to the first AA meeting they returned home laughing over what happened. As they walked through the door before the meeting started, several people greeted my husband, shaking his hand and clapping him on the back, making him feel welcome.

It was evident from their remarks they thought Amy was accompanying her father to his first AA meeting. A few weeks later, there were surprised looks throughout the room when she walked to the front to receive her three-month-sober coin. Another reminder that alcoholism knows no age.

Amy volunteered at Peterborough Pregnancy Support Services for several years. God blessed her with opportunities to share her testimony and counsel women who were considering an abortion. She found it heart-wrenching to talk about her past, but the joy of sharing what Jesus did for her gave her the courage to do what she felt God had called her to do.

I commend my daughter for her willingness to share her story. It took a great deal of courage to expose the hidden details of her sinful life, first to us and then to you, our readers. I am proud of the godly woman our daughter is today.

God had a surprise waiting for the young woman who said she'd never get married. She met Stephen, a talented and dedicated musician from our church who plays electric guitar and drums. He is part of the worship team and ministers with the band in our Sunday services. Amy and Stephen were married three years later at Calvary Pentecostal Church by Pastor Patrick and Pastor Morris in a beautiful winter wedding.

We are once again empty-nesters. Bill looks forward to retirement in a few years and I continue to write and work in my garden. With three adorable grandchildren—Adam, Naomi and Nathan—we are enjoying all the delights of being grandparents.

This book is a testimony of God's story intersecting with ours. His story is the one we hope you will remember. We encourage parents and teenagers to read it together. It is our desire and prayer that it will open doors for honest communication and give you the courage to take off your masks—masks of pain, grief, brokenness, despair, shame, anger, and resentment—masks we all hide behind.

We humbly offer this story as an encouragement to those whose wayward children have not yet come home. For you, dear parents, feeling alone and misunderstood, staggering under a crushing load of guilt and despair, there is hope. It is only found in Jesus. May this book help point you to the One who loves you with an unfailing love. He will hold your hand when you feel discouraged, fill your aching heart with hope, and protect you in his loving embrace—safe and secure through all the storms of life.

You are not alone. Many hurting families in our churches are experiencing dark days that never seem to end. Take heart. There are caring, compassionate people in the family of God who will encourage and comfort you when you find the courage to share your story. Together we will support each other in love and prayer, and trust in the mercy of our God until all of our prodigals come home.

May all our family circles be unbroken.

AMY

It's when we think we have the answers. It's when we are tired of hearing about the right way. It's when we are sure that we've done enough good things. It's at those times that the enemy of our soul launches his attack. You see, it's then that you let your guard down, when you're sure you know yourself, when you're sure you know what you will and will not do. It's at that point, the point where you've heard the right teaching for so long you feel indestructible. At what you think is your 'strongest' moment, the Devil begins to shoot his arrows of rationalization and justification—arrows that pierce the skin, and if left, fester and infect.

I thought I was happy. I thought just believing what my parents believed was enough. I thought I knew who I was and what I wanted. But I didn't, how could I? How can the creation tell the Creator who they are? I thought I knew, but really I just kept slipping lower and lower ignoring the person that I had become, piling sin on top of sin, from the very start.

Then Jesus broke all my chains, everything that held me hostage. All those things that I swore I couldn't live without, he abolished! Looking back now I never thought I'd be able to quit. Quit the drugs, quit the sex, quit the drinking, quit the lie my life had become.

You have taught me, Lord, that I can't change myself on my own. All I can do is want to change. All I can do is seek you. The actual power to change comes from you, Jesus. Never in my life have I known such inexpressible joy; joy that cannot compare to any drug. Knowing there is a God, a God who loves me so much he took the punishment I deserved that I may be called his child—it's almost unbelievable! Jesus Christ you have changed my life drastically. You are my freedom! I'm no longer a slave trapped in the chains of alcohol, drugs, and sex. I'm set free from condemnation.

I've come to Him a dirty, decaying, sinful mess and he has cleansed me! I've come to him a lonely, hurt and confused person and he has given me mercy and love. I've come to him a lost little girl and he has given my life a purpose. All that I did was come to him, he did the rest!

"Therefore, if anyone is in Christ, he is a new creation;
the old has gone, the new has come!"

2 Corinthians 5:17

AFTERWORD

SHARON

The idea for this book initially came from a comment my daughter made one day after she finished her alcohol-education course and AA meetings. "We should write about this," she said. We looked at each other and laughed. She didn't know I'd been thinking the same thing. For a long time the seed of that idea lay buried in my mind.

At the time, I had a pile of writing projects waiting on my desk. They had been sitting on hold long enough, now I needed to finish them. But God had other plans. Over the next few years, he brought the idea of writing our story to my attention in numerous ways. Every conference I attended, every sermon preached, every special speaker, every book I picked all conveyed the same message in some way: If God has done something amazing in your life, share it with others. You have a story to tell.

One morning after church, a gentleman came to speak to Bill and me. "You don't know me, but I felt lead to come and talk to you." He paused as tears filled his eyes. "I'm a pastor in another city and my son is far away from God." He shared with us the terrible pain and heartbreak he lived with because of the broken relationship with his prodigal son.

We were able to tell him of our own prodigal daughter and the struggles we faced. I think it helped him to know he was not alone. We prayed with him, assuring him we would continue to remember his son in prayer. Together we acknowledged that nothing is impossible with God. He thanked us and left, his face wet with tears. My heart ached for him. I understood his pain.

A few days later, I called Amy. "I can't get away from the idea that we should write our story together. God keeps bringing it to my mind." She told me she had been thinking about it too. Over the years, I'd written other people's stories and always enjoyed reading biographies, but telling our own story seemed a daunting task.

We learned a lot about each other as we worked on the book. It shocked me to discover that we were each living in our own separate reality. I wondered how many other parents and young people were doing the same. Living in the same house, eating meals together, maybe even going to church together while all the time their individual lives were disconnected and hidden from each another.

I overheard a mother say, "I never have to worry about my kids. They know they can talk to me about anything, and I know they always do. We are a close family. We have no secrets from each other." I felt the same, but I was sadly mistaken.

The pages of my journals provided abundant proof of God's faithfulness. We saw the connection between the times God burdened our hearts to pray for Amy and her desperate need of God's intervention in her life. People were earnestly praying for us—Amy's grandparents Herman and Winnie Cox, Jean Cavers, family members, and many dear friends in our church family. I believe those fervent prayers had a direct impact on our daughter's life.

Through the pages of the book we watched her stumbling steps toward Abba Father's welcoming arms. He picked up the broken pieces of Amy's life and made them into something beautiful. She came to Jesus dirty, wounded and broken, and his redeeming grace transformed a rebel into a child of God.

The sharing of our story has often been a painful process as we relived our darkest moments. As parents, we recognized our many mistakes. Jo March said it best in Little Women, "I'm hopelessly flawed." I saw with new eyes how my fears and, at times, my flagging faith kept me from fully trusting God. Through it all we found our hope and strength and wisdom in him. There is no other source of Life.

NOTES

PROLOGUE

1. We, the authors, are convinced there is a real spiritual entity which the Bible calls the "Devil" or "Satan". He is called the father of lies, the accuser and the enemy (of all mankind and God). He is actively attempting to deceive and destroy every person God has ever created and convince them of whatever will prevent them from trusting and believing in God and faith in Jesus Christ.

CHAPTER ONE
BEGINNINGS

2. 2 Kings 4:16

CHAPTER TWO
CHANGES

3. Tim LaHaye explains the different temperaments in *Why You Act The Way You Do* (Wheaton: Tyndale House Publishers, Inc., 1984).

CHAPTER FOUR
CHAMELEON

4. Psalm 56:3

CHAPTER SIX
CONFRONTATION

5. Dr. James Dobson, *On Parenting* (The Strong-willed Child & Parenting Isn't for Cowards) First Inspirational Press edition published in 1997. Published by arrangement with Tyndale House Publishers and Word Inc., 415

CHAPTER SEVEN
THE PATH OF REBELLION

6. Daniel 6:17

7. Franklin Graham, *Rebel With A Cause* (Nashville: Thomas Nelson, Inc., 1995), 115.

CHAPTER EIGHT
PRAYING FOR A ROADBLOCK

8. Mark 9:24

CHAPTER NINE
FAKE FREEDOM

9. Adaptation of a quote by Matthew Henry, *Matthew Henry Commentary on the Whole Bible* (1710), Psalm 58.

CHAPTER TEN
LETTING GO

10. Joel 2:25, KJV
11. Joel 2:28, KJV

CHAPTER ELEVEN
OUT OF CONTROL

12. *Just as I Am,* text by Charlotte Elliot, music by William B. Bradbury

CHAPTER THIRTEEN
CONFESSION

13. Judges 13:25
14. Isaiah 59:19, KJV

CHAPTER FOURTEEN
LISTENING

15. Isaiah 33:6
16. Romans 7:15, my paraphrase
17. *I Miss The Way,* songwriters: Michael W. Smith and Wayne Kirkpatrick © 1988
18. 2 Timothy 1:5

CHAPTER FIFTEEN
LOVING UNCONDITIONALLY

19. Psalm 112: 1,4,7

CHAPTER SIXTEEN
ANCHORED IN THE STORM

20. Isaiah 40:31

CHAPTER NINETEEN
IN GOD'S HANDS

21. Philippians 4:6, The Message
22. Philippians 4:7, The Message

CHAPTER TWENTY
FACING THE TRUTH

23. Genesis 37:11

CHAPTER TWENTY TWO
ONE STEP FORWARD TWO STEPS BACK

24. C.S. Lewis, *The Problem of Pain* (New York: HarperCollins Publishers, 1940), 91.

CHAPTER TWENTY THREE
TRADITIONS

25. Proverbs 14:26
26. Luke 2:19, The Message

CHAPTER TWENTY FOUR
WARFARE

27. Psalm 27:14
28. Proverbs 13:12
29. Psalm 119:176

CHAPTER TWENTY SEVEN
CELEBRATING GOD'S FAITHFULNESS

30. Author unknown

31. Thomas Obadiah Chisholm, letter dated 1941, Amazing Hymn Stories, www.tanbible.com/tol_sng/greatisthyfaithfulness.htm

CHAPTER TWENTY NINE
WHAT DO WE DO NOW, LORD?

32. Genesis 50:20

33. Philippians 4:19

34. Proverbs 3: 5,6

CHAPTER THIRTY TWO
TRUSTING GOD IN THE DARK

35. James 4:7

36. Lamentations 3:25,26

CHAPTER THIRTY THREE
PEACE OF MIND

37. Psalm 56:8, TLB

38. *Blessed Be Your Name*, words and music by Matt Redman and Beth Redman

Dear readers,

Thank you for choosing our book. Our prayer is that you have been encouraged and reminded of God's faithfulness. Never give up hope. Nothing is impossible with God.

We would love to hear from you.

scavers@craigfoster.com
amycavers@hotmail.com

LaVergne, TN USA
15 December 2010
208768LV00002B/2/P